NADIA WASSEF

SHELF LIFE

Nadia Wassef is one of the owners of Diwan, Egypt's first modern bookstore, which she cofounded in 2002. She holds three master's degrees: an MA in creative writing from Birkbeck, University of London, an MA in social anthropology from the School of Oriental and African Studies at the University of London, and an MA in English and comparative literature from the American University in Cairo. Before cofounding Diwan, she worked in research and advocacy for the Female Genital Mutilation Task Force and the Women and Memory Forum. She was featured on the *Forbes Middle East* list of the two hundred most powerful Arab women in the Middle East in 2014, 2015, and 2016, and her work has been covered in *Time*, *Monocle*, and *Business Monthly*, among other publications. She lives in London with her two daughters.

SHELF LIFE

SHELF
LIFE

———◆———

CHRONICLES
OF A
CAIRO
BOOKSELLER

NADIA WASSEF

PICADOR

FARRAR, STRAUS AND GIROUX

NEW YORK

Picador
120 Broadway, New York 10271

Originally published in 2021 by Farrar, Straus and Giroux
First paperback edition, 2022

Chapter-opening illustration by Drawlab19 / shutterstock.com.

The Library of Congress has cataloged the Farrar, Straus and Giroux
hardcover edition as follows:
Names: Wassef, Nadia, author.   ⋮
Title: Shelf life : chronicles of a Cairo bookseller / Nadia Wassef.
Description: First edition. | New York : Farrar, Straus and Giroux, 2021.
Identifiers: LCCN 2021020108 | ISBN 9780374600181 (hardcover)
Subjects: LCSH: Wassef, Nadia. | Booksellers and bookselling—Egypt—
    Cairo—Biography. | Diwan (Bookstore : Zamalek, Cairo, Egypt) |
    Bookstores—Egypt—Cairo.
Classification: LCC Z466.E43 W37 2021 | DDC 381/.45002092—dc23
LC record available at https://lccn.loc.gov/2021020108

Paperback ISBN: 978-1-250-85886-3

Our books may be purchased in bulk for promotional, educational,
or business use. Please contact your local bookseller or the Macmillan
Corporate and Premium Sales Department at 1-800-221-7945, extension
5442, or by email at MacmillanSpecialMarkets@macmillan.com.

Picador® is a U.S. registered trademark and is used by Macmillan
Publishing Group, LLC, under license from Pan Books Limited.

For book club information, please visit facebook.com/picadorbookclub or
email marketing@picadorusa.com.

picadorusa.com · instagram.com/picador
twitter.com/picadorusa · facebook.com/picadorusa

P1

For Ramzi and Faiza, who made it all possible.

For Hind, who hears every heartbeat.

For Zein and Layla. I did my best.

This is a true story, though some names have been changed.

CONTENTS

———◆———

SHELF LIFE

PROLOGUE

I was seven years old when members of the Muslim Brotherhood assassinated Anwar Sadat, and his vice president, Hosni Mubarak, took over, in 1981. I was a thirty-seven-year-old bookseller with ten bookstores, 150 employees, two master's degrees, one ex-husband (from here on known as Number One), one second husband (Number Two), and two daughters, when Mubarak was removed from power in 2011.

But our story begins long before the Egyptian revolution, and before the series of uprisings known as the Arab Spring. For most of my life, I have lived in Zamalek, a neighborhood on an island in a river surrounded by a desert: coordinates thirty degrees north, thirty-one degrees east. Zamalek, a district of western Cairo, reclines in the middle of the Nile. Legend has it that Cairo is named after the planet Mars, Al-Najm Al-Qahir, which was rising on the day the city was founded. She is known as al-Qahira, the feminine for "vanquisher."

On Zamalek's main pedestrian and traffic artery, 26th of July Street, stand two sister buildings called the Baehler mansions. Their high ceilings, courtyards, and stucco flourishes suggest a glorious past. Air-conditioning compressors tenaciously cling to balcony railings, loose cables collect dirt and scraps of paper, and laundry hangs in the heat. A string of businesses lines the street: Nouby, the antiques dealer; Cilantro, the coffee shop; Thomas Pizza; the Bank of Alexandria; and a windowed corner store, Diwan—the bookstore that my sister, Hind, and I founded in March 2002. In the years after, Hind and I opened sixteen locations (and closed six) across Egypt, but each one of our stores emulates the look and feel of this one, our flagship, our firstborn.

Hind and I conceived of Diwan one night in 2001, over dinner with our old friends Ziad, Nihal, and Nihal's then husband, Ali. Someone posed the question: If you could do anything, what would you do? Hind and I offered the same answer. We would open a bookstore, the first of its kind in Cairo. Our father had died recently from a merciless motor neuron disease. As lifelong readers, we had turned to books for solace—but our city lacked modern bookstores. In Egypt at the turn of the millennium, publishing, distribution, and bookselling were worn-out from decades of socialism gone awry. Beginning under the rule of Gamal Abdel Nasser, the second president of Egypt, through Anwar Sadat (the third) and then Hosni Mubarak (the fourth), the state's failure to address the population boom led to illiteracy, corruption, and diminished infrastructure. In an effort to suppress dissent, each political regime had taken control of cultural output. Writers became government employees; literature died many successive slow and bureaucratic deaths. Few people in Egypt seemed interested in reading or writing. Starting a bookstore at this moment of cultural atrophy seemed impossible—and utterly necessary. To our surprise, our dinner companions were equally interested. That night, we became five business partners: Ziad, Ali, Nihal, Hind, and me. In the months that followed, we discussed, networked, and planned incessantly. Then, Hind, Nihal, and

I got to work. And it was through that shared toil that we became chosen sisters, the three women of Diwan.

As people, Hind, Nihal, and I could not have been more different. Hind is private and fiercely loyal, Nihal is spiritual and generous, and I'm a doer. As business partners, we tried to be better versions of ourselves, failing more often than not. We divided work based on preference and passion: Hind and I were best with books, and Nihal was best with people. These divisions were never clear-cut. We all found common ground in language. We devoted our attention and our labor to words. We were proud of Egyptian culture and eager to share it. We had no business plan, no warehouse, and no fear. We were unburdened by our lack of qualifications, and we were ignorant of all the challenges that lay ahead. We were young women—I was twenty-seven, Hind was thirty, and Nihal was forty. Over the next two decades, we would hold one another's hands through marriages, divorces, births, and deaths. We would confront the difficulties of running a business in a patriarchal society: navigating harassment and discrimination, cajoling bureaucratic despots, and becoming fluent in Egypt's censorship laws in the process.

From the beginning, we knew that our bookstore couldn't be a relic of the past. It had to have a purpose and a vision. Every aspect had to be intentional, beginning with the name. One afternoon, our mother, Faiza, listened politely as Hind and I grappled with this dilemma. Underwhelmed by our suggestions, and eager to return to her lunch, she proposed "Diwan." She enumerated its translations: a collection of poetry in Persian and Arabic, a meeting place, a guesthouse, a sofa, and a title for high-ranking officials. "Diwani" was a type of Arabic calligraphy. She paused, then added that the word worked phonetically in Arabic,

English, and French. She returned to the plate in front of her. We were dismissed.

Empowered by our name, we approached Nermine Hammam, a graphic designer also known as Minou, to help us build our brand. Her humor was swift and biting, her gummy smile all-knowing. Minou asked Hind, Nihal, and me to describe Diwan as if she were a person. We told her that she *was* a person, and this was her story:

> Diwan was conceived as a reaction to a world that had stopped caring about the written word. She was born on March 8, 2002—coincidentally, International Women's Day. She is larger than the space she occupies. She welcomes and respects others in all their differences. Like a good host, she invites patrons to stay a while longer in her café. In principle, she is anti-smoking; she knows that most places in her homeland aren't, but she is resolved to stand for better. She has nobler ideals than her surroundings permit. She is honest, but she will not punish thieves. She is sincere, and insists on weeding out those who aren't. She doesn't like numbers. She doesn't like the binary world that surrounds her, and she is set on changing it, one book at a time. She believes that North and South, East and West are restrictive terms, so she offers books in Arabic, English, French, and German. She brings people and ideas together.

Minou translated our description into a logo. She wrote D-I-W-A in an eccentric black font, adding the "N" in Arabic. This last letter—a nod to nuun al-niswa and nuun al-inath—

genders verbs, adjectives, and nouns to the feminine. Minou surrounded the entire word with tashkeel, or diacritics.

Not only did Minou design a logo, she created a brand that could grow and change. She invented ways for Diwan to spread: bags, bookmarks, cards, candles, wrapping paper, pens, pencils, and wallpaper. The Diwan shopping bag became a cultural status symbol on the streets of Cairo. In later years, when I glimpsed one of our bags on a London street, or a New York subway, the feeling was electrifying.

In the two years following the revolution, as the Muslim Brotherhood rose to power, Cairo transformed into something almost unrecognizable—and I began to consider leaving. The prospect was extremely painful, but after years of running Diwan in postrevolutionary chaos, I was running on empty. I'd begun to realize that as long as I stayed in Cairo, I existed only in relation to my bookstores. I could never extricate myself. And after fourteen years of giving myself to the shop, I had to draw a line in the sand—I surrendered my role as one of Diwan's managers. After a brief stint in Dubai with Number Two, Zein (now sixteen), Layla (now fourteen), and I moved to London. While I no longer manage Diwan—Nihal took over—I keep returning to those years in my mind, feeling some mix of longing and relief.

Hind, my soul mate and my savior, never speaks about that time; she has chosen silence over reminiscence.

Diwan was my love letter to Egypt. It was part of, and fueled, my search for myself, my Cairo, my country. And this book is my love letter to Diwan. Each chapter maps a section of the bookstore, from the café to the self-help section, and the people who frequented them: the coworkers, the regulars, the floaters, the thieves, the friends, and the family who called Diwan home. Those of us who write love letters know that their aims are impossible. We try, and fail, to make the ethereal material. We strive against the inevitable ending, knowing that everything is transient. We choose to be grateful for the time, however brief it may be.

1

THE CAFÉ

To the uninitiated pedestrian, Diwan was just one of several shops behind the Baehler mansions' ornate exterior. The traditional royal-blue street sign read *Shari' 26 Yulyu*, 26th of July Street. We'd placed our logo, in formidable black text, on the building's façade. A supplicant jacaranda bowed over the shop entrance. The glass front door, which faced the street corner, was adorned with modern Arabo-Islamic designs and a long silver handle.

Inside was an oasis from the hot, traffic-choked street. Strains of Arabo-jazz, Umm Kulthum, and George Gershwin were underscored by the mechanical din of air-conditioning units. Beneath a mighty wall with signs for recommendations, bestsellers, and new releases, Arabic and English fiction and nonfiction books cascaded from floating shelves. Visitors could either walk through the doorway on the right to the book section, past the cashier and stationery, or enter the left doorway into the multimedia section, a curated collection of boundary-crossing film and music: experimental and classic, Eastern and Western.

During the research phase of setting up Diwan, I'd read an article stating that most people turn right upon entering a bookstore. Swayed by this observation, we placed the book section of Diwan to the right. There, the windows looked out onto the adjoining courtyard rather than the main road, making it the quieter part of the store. High ceilings lined with tracks of incandescent lighting illuminated mahogany wood shelves with a matte-steel trim—a marriage of old and new. The books were split into two categories. On the left were our Arabic books, which Hind stocked. On the right were the English books: my domain. We placed our modest selection of French and German titles in the multimedia section. A nearby entryway led to the café, the central hearth of the store.

Customer-service staff circulated through the rooms dressed in Diwan uniforms: a navy-blue polo shirt with our logo stitched in beige on the left-hand side, and beige pants with the pockets sewn shut to prevent theft. They offered their knowledge, trying to strike a balance between eagerness and professional distance. Their job was more demanding than that of booksellers elsewhere, especially when we first opened, when most customers were completely unfamiliar with Diwan's approach.

I understood their confusion.

Before Diwan, there had been three kinds of Egyptian bookshops: those mismanaged by the government; those affiliated with particular publishing houses; and the small local shops, which primarily sold newspapers and stationery. The government bookshops left the strongest impression on me. As a university student, I used to take taxis to Cairo's city center, where the Armenians once ran guilds; the Italians, department stores; and the Greeks, groceries. I would travel along the main roads of my city, all named after dates of historical significance. (26th of July Street was formerly called Fouad I, after the first king of modern Egypt. It was renamed for the day Fouad's son, Farouk, left the country on his royal yacht, during the 1952 revolution

future. We were on the verge of an artistic and cultural renaissance—even though we still lacked basic modern amenities. Like bookstores.

Hind helped us ride this wave by solving problems early and often. She visited other bookstores and publishers, taking note of what they offered and asking questions. On these scouting missions, Hind made herself small, subdued, and unthreatening. Other business owners met her inquiries with skeptical and sometimes patronizing responses; she remained unfazed. While speaking to a publishing manager, she discovered that few locally printed book jackets carried ISBNs (an International Standard Book Number identifies every published book). In Egypt, ISBNs were generated one at a time by national libraries, which granted approval only to titles that didn't antagonize the prevailing government. Independent publishers creatively evaded censorship by forgoing the ISBN altogether or "borrowing" the ISBNs of already published titles. Egyptian authors sometimes published in other countries. The absence of those numbers meant that the process of invoicing, dispatching, and tracking books was subject to serious margins of error. National bestseller lists couldn't be compiled. Back at Diwan, Hind faced this hellish realization with characteristic patience. She created a manual for transliterating authors' names and titles into our English-language-based computer system, which covered every probable formation. By adopting this phonetic system, we were able to generate house codes for our Arabic books.

Then, she ventured into the great unknown: sales figures. Bookstores in Egypt had traditionally used manual registers or handwritten receipts. No one knew precisely what they were selling, so no one knew how to stock well. Anyone who did track sales figures kept them secret. Hind defied convention by compiling these numbers and then publishing Diwan's bestseller lists, inciting competition between publishers and authors and introducing readers to new books. This was just the beginning. I never really knew of Hind's plans until after she'd succeeded in them. We both shared a belief that doing preceded talking.

Cairo's depleted bookselling industry had fostered two primary types of readers: those resigned to the broken system, and those, like Hind, Nihal, and I, who wanted an alternative. Diwan's customers held an array of assumptions and attitudes about bookstores. It was our job to detect, and sometimes dispel, their biases. Seasoned readers found their haven here: buying new and selling used books, recommending new titles, and participating in the wider conversation. They personally sought out us owners to discuss errors in customer service and share grievances. They were eager for Diwan to succeed and maintain its standards. To this day, I receive emails and messages on social media from customers who are upset about shipping delays or other issues. Some still want one of the founding partners to personally oversee a sale.

Others had less benevolent intentions.

A typical interaction went like this. "I demand to speak to the owner," a customer would say, marching up to Nihal, Hind, or me.

"I'm one of them," Nihal or Hind would respond. I always tried to recede into the background, busying myself with some suddenly pressing task.

"I need to return this book."

"I'm sorry to hear that. Is there something wrong with it?"

"I bought it. I read it. I don't like it. I want my money back."

From here, the exchange differed based on the listener. Nihal would always nod, helping the customer feel heard. She'd kindly explain that Diwan was not a library. Frequently, the customer would respond and say that we should be one. Wasn't culture a shared resource? At this stage, unable to control myself, I'd jump in, saying how this backward belief was what had gotten us where we were in Egypt—until, after many similar interactions, I finally learned to hold my tongue. Nihal would gently direct customers toward the many government-run libraries that could fulfill their needs, all the while commiserating that Diwan didn't follow the same model. In her encounters, Hind, who had a taste for the absurd, would engage in extensive discussions to test the limits of these customers' logic. In polite tones of faux naïveté, she would disprove their arguments with a debater's agility. If the conversation grew tedious, she would look at her watch and politely excuse herself. Hind is the least punctual person I know. Like my mother, she has a quiet ruthlessness and an ability to subtly dismiss a person if she no longer has time for them.

Other customers were kinder, even as they struggled to navigate this foreign terrain. They'd admire the cleanliness, the meticulous attention to detail, the décor, the staff, and then mount the same challenge: Why was this a store and not a library? Hind, Nihal, and I—forever present on the shop floor—pointed out that a library couldn't sustain the costs of rent, salaries, uniforms, taxes, and the host of other expenditures small businesses contend with. When we were inevitably asked if Diwan was part of Mrs. Mubarak's literacy initiative, we would reply that it had nothing to do with the First Lady or the government—this was a private endeavor. They'd respond with surprise: Why would any sane person invest money in the losing venture of bookselling?

Even before we opened Diwan, our venture met with disbelief. During our research phase, Ali, Nihal's husband and one of our cofounders, suggested we interview writers about where they bought their books. An alum of the Deutsche Evangelische Oberschule, one of Cairo's German schools, Ali was an avid reader and a people person with an infectious laugh. I marveled at his ability to spark friendships, and maintain them, across generations, continents, and ideologies. One afternoon, we accompanied him on a meeting with one of Egypt's eminent journalists. As the journalist listened to Hind's and my pitch, he looked us up and down. Finally, the journalist issued his verdict: we were bourgeois housewives wasting our time and money. Since the demise of the middle class, people in Egypt didn't read anymore.

"But do things need to be financially sustainable to exist?" I asked the journalist. "Governments maintain public spaces like gardens, museums, libraries, to better the cultural health of nations. So why do you condemn individuals to failure when they go on similar missions?"

"You are young women with no experience of the world. I speak to you as I would to my children. I'm trying to spare you the disappointment. You don't know the challenges that going into business entails, let alone if that business is based on reading. You will be eaten alive by your suppliers and your clients."

Never mind my disappointment, I thought to myself—what about Egypt's? What happens to countries that neglect their cultural projects in favor of dams and highways? The answer was clear to see. Our museums had become graveyards, dead spaces devoted to the triumphs of a few strongmen. Our schoolbooks echoed these lies and omissions. The journalist believed that culture had become a preoccupation of the elite, and that books were irrelevant to people who were fighting to stay above the poverty line. He wasn't wrong. But we had to believe in our store and our books. If we Egyptians became alienated from who we were, we'd never know who we could be.

Diwan emerged onto this cultural landscape, standing directly at the crossroads of the present and the past. Nihal designed the café accordingly, adapting the intimate tearooms of Quiberon, in western France, where she'd spent summers, for Cairo's bustle. She approached aesthetics with her trademark fairness, pairing marble-topped tables with wooden-and-chrome chairs. The chairs were a compromise—she'd initially wanted more comfortable seating, but Hind thought that that would limit client turnover. Variations of cappuccinos, Turkish coffees, and infusions of chamomile, hibiscus, cinnamon, and mint were listed on one side of the menu; on the other, cheese pâtés, doughy pizzas, slices of carrot cake, brownies, and chocolate chip cookies. Knives and forks, wrapped in napkins bearing Diwan's logo, stood at the ready. Hassan, the principal server, was a Sudanese refugee with a stutter who frequently lost his temper with clients who didn't understand his enunciation. Nihal appreciated his smile as well as his rigorous hygiene standards. Through her coaxing of both Hassan and the clientele, customers grew used to Hassan, and Hassan grew into his words.

Graceful mediation came naturally to Nihal, who was the youngest of three sisters and yet somehow the most maternal of us. I waited to witness a situation where Nihal didn't get her way—I'm still waiting. She's the only person I know who fasts the entire month of Ramadan without complaining once. We have managed to argue for two decades, and forgive each other for two decades.

Nihal's disposition uniquely prepared her for the eclectic characters and behaviors that mingled in our seemingly chaste café. Like most spaces, it had a mind of its own, regardless of what we called it. I remember applying for a license for Diwan. I told the bureaucrat at the municipality office that we would sell books, films, music, and stationery, and that we would have a café. He gave me a blank stare. "You can't," he said in a bored tone, not raising his head from the form in front of him.

"Why not?" I questioned, lacing defiance with naïveté, hoping he would engage with me.

"A space can only be licensed for one activity. You can't be a bank and a school. Pick one."

"Can't I be a teacher by day and a belly dancer by night?" I asked.

He gave a halfhearted smile. "Someone with two mindsets is a liar," he said, quoting a popular saying to terminate our discussion.

"And we're a bookstore," I declared. He sighed, filled in the last line on the form, stamped it with faded blue ink, and handed it back to me, all without glancing up from the next form on his desk. I withheld my final retort: we are a bookstore where people will spend not only money, but time.

One cruel irony of Egypt in the latter half of the twentieth century: just as people began to have more free time, the physical spaces designed for recreation began to shrink.

Urban development encroached on city parks. Promenades and cafés along the banks of the Nile were turned into private clubs for army officers and government syndicates. The "public sphere," a spatial and theoretical concept introduced by the German philosopher Jürgen Habermas, was in transition. Habermas's public sphere describes the social arenas in which people gather to share ideas, where private individuals enter into a collective. The term informed the sociologist Ray Oldenburg's theory of the "third place" (after home, the first place, and work, the second). Third places are locations for community building, which, by his definition, include cafés, like ours. In Egypt, men had their mosques, barbershops, and the *ahwa*—coffee shops where they smoked *sheesha*, played backgammon and dominoes, listened to the radio, and watched the television and the world go by. Young men had their sports clubs. Women had their homes, which they rarely owned.

Men are defined by what they do, and women, by their intimate relationships. Take Ada Lovelace. Even though she was a renowned mathematician and the world's first computer programmer, she's probably just as famous for being Byron's daughter. A few years after we founded the shop, customers, friends, and acquaintances began calling me "Mrs. Diwan." I'd begun spending all my time at Diwan. I dreamed of Diwan. I was at my desk by eight o'clock most mornings and left well into the evening. I wanted to overlap with the morning and afternoon shifts, as well as make sure that staff in the head office knew that I would be there when they arrived and after they left. And when I wasn't there, I was thinking about Diwan. It was true that my identity had gradually become indistinguishable from the store's, in a way that threatened my relationship with Number

One—but more on that later. Still, I bristled at the idea that even in my sobriquet, Diwan was positioned as "the man," making me subservient to the very thing I'd created.

Bookstores are both private and public spaces, in which we escape the world and also participate in it more fully. Our café in particular held these contradictions: a place where friends gathered, where people lingered for hours (despite the chairs), where I often brought my daughters on the weekends. A place that resembled a home but that wasn't a home. Prior to becoming Diwan, the whole shop had been a testosterone-filled gym called Sports Palace. I savored the irony of our female-owned-and-operated bookstore replacing that temple of masculinity.

Hind and I had grown up in a world that constantly excluded us; it neither belonged to us nor granted us belonging. As kids, most mornings, we would leave our home at seven thirty and walk down the muted marble corridor to the elevators. I would press the button over and over—out of impatience, and disbelief that the elevator had registered my request. I hated the steel cuboid with neon lights that had replaced the original Schindler wooden compartment, with its foldable miniature banquette and bronze, crystal-domed ceiling light, but going down four flights of marble that were coated in soapy water from the morning cleaner seemed ill-advised. A hospital-like tone announced the elevator's arrival. Most mornings, the left panel slid into the right to reveal one of our neighbors from the floor above: an older gentleman, with a lit cigarette between his lips. We would enter the matte-silver compartment, watching the rings of smoke, holding our breath in protest. If I had been a man, would he have extinguished his cigarette on the floor the moment I entered? The elevator nodded into place on the ground floor. As soon as the doors opened, we pushed our way out, past a fresh puff.

I remember one formative conversation I had with my father when I was a teenager. Following some long-forgotten infraction, I complained to him about this world, the world I was beginning to understand kept women in their place. He drew my attention to the next world: in the Muslim promise of heaven, houris—beautiful virgins—are offered as rewards to pious men.

"It's a man's world. Change it on your own time, but until then, learn to deal with it," my father suggested with gruff pragmatism.

"How can heaven be so exclusionist? Why should I even try to be good if all I end up with is a bunch of virgins?" I cried.

"You aren't the target audience," my father said, laughing at the world he glimpsed through my eyes.

"God's bestseller has half the world as a captive audience, that's the problem."

"As always, you are misdiagnosing the problem." He placed his rectangular glasses on the rim of his nose, picked up the newspaper, and resumed his reading, with one afterthought: "Maybe one day you can push other bestsellers."

We decided to make Diwan a space that catered to us, rather than the other way around. Soon, other women began to find respite in Diwan—a home away from the burdens of home, a public place less fraught with the pressures of being a woman in public, where we are constantly reminded of our nonexistence. Public toilets in Egypt were normally attached to mosques or churches. The state offered few other alternatives. Men were free to urinate under flyovers or against the sides of buildings. Women's toilets in public spaces were putrid-smelling holes in the ground, flooded by running taps. Soap and toilet paper were never available, and no one expected them to be. It was this reality that brought to Diwan an entire cross-section of women who were not necessarily readers but who found relief at the end of its winding corridors: it became their toilet on 26th of July Street. Few shops had facilities, and if they did, the proprietors were not inclined to share them. Diwan was more gracious. And the café, with its book-covered walls, became a makeshift barrier between women and their harassers, men who knew that we, the women of Diwan, wouldn't tolerate their hostility.

Diwan's café served numerous purposes and patrons. Ardent readers browsed through the pile of books they had collected before making their selection. Visitors came to idle away a portion of their days, while others made it their gathering place, catching up with old friends or acquaintances they didn't want to host at home. Gray economies unfolded over the marble-topped tables: people had their astrological charts or fortunes read, while nearby, private tutors coaxed reluctant pupils.

"She's back at her usual table. In four hours, she has consumed one Turkish coffee and a bottle of water," said Nihal one day, with a hint of irritation.

"Did she buy any books?" asked Hind.

"No. She's just here to tutor. People like her don't leave space for our regulars."

"The customer-service staff suggested we impose a minimum charge," I said, testing the waters.

"Absolutely not! You can't charge people for sitting in a space that you created to serve them," said Nihal, her eyes wide with shock.

"You can't ask for a commission on the lessons, so what else do you propose?"

"You built it. *They* came. Make the drinks more expensive, the chairs less comfortable, or the music more disruptive. Find a way to impose your business model onto theirs," Hind said curtly, heading toward the Arabic book display. I avoided Nihal's plaintive stare. As a control freak, I sympathized: How could we tailor a space to its designated purpose without evicting its occupants?

One young patron sat in the café almost every evening. She seldom read our books, instead passing the time scribbling into a leather-bound journal. I wondered what she did by day. In my mind, I named her Pavlova, since she had the guileless allure of a ballerina. Her hair was usually pulled into a bun, but sometimes she let it hang down her back. And in her eyes, there was a look of distance, of a soul displaced from the body it inhabited. We communicated via polite nods.

"You know the lady who sits in the café, your ballerina?" said Shahira, her lips pursed. Shahira was one of our earliest, and longest-standing, managers, a feisty young woman whose power extended well beyond her deceptively modest frame. Before her, we'd had a series of managers who'd quit within weeks of getting hired, overwhelmed by balancing the needs of staff, customers, and Cairo's flaneurs simultaneously. Not Shahira.

"Yes, of course. Who upset her?" I asked, putting down my glasses and preparing to make amends.

"No one. One of the cleaning staff complained that she doesn't wear underwear, so he is forced to view things he doesn't want to. Apparently, she works all of 26th of July Street, and Diwan is her new fishing ground."

"Surely not," I said, faltering a bit as I considered the parade of eccentrics who used the café as their living room.

"I'll monitor her and get back to you. If it's true, we need to put an end to it," Shahira said. I didn't want it to be true. And if it was, I didn't want to deal with it. Pavlova continued to frequent Diwan, but our polite nods became briefer. Her visits incited louder whispers from my staff. That week, Shahira had tea and gossiped with neighboring shopkeepers, gathering details of Pavlova's interactions. Each one confirmed her suspicions. After hearing the news, I took my time, waiting for a quiet evening when business was slow and the audience was minimal. Finally, I approached Pavlova's table. She looked up at me. I opened my mouth to speak, unsure of how to acknowledge what I knew.

"I'm told that you don't like our coffee. Can I suggest one of the other coffee shops next to us?" I smiled politely.

"You must be misinformed. I like it fine here." She didn't return my smile. I hesitated, and then my words found their momentum.

"I mean no offense. We all work for a living, and work is to be respected. But could you kindly conduct your business elsewhere? You're no longer welcome here. Please don't come back." I retreated, not wanting to witness the impact of my remarks. The following morning, Shahira asked how it went. I commented that our staff gossiped too much. Shahira was undeterred, so I recounted my exchange with Pavlova.

"Why do you feel guilty? She's the one taking advantage of us."

When Pavlova was little, I'm sure she didn't look up at the sky and wish that when she grew up, she'd be working

26th of July Street. We allowed people to offer other services, like tutoring, in our café, but because Pavlova's work was sexual, we acted self-righteous. Were we right to be so moralistic? I thought about the third space we'd created, a public place where intensely private interactions unfolded. In books, gestures, coffee cups, and tea leaves, we all searched for ourselves, each other, and a means for survival. A few days later, on my walk back home, I spotted Pavlova sitting in the upstairs window of a coffee shop nearby. Her legs swayed in a loose, frilly skirt.

Diwan's café doubled as our office before we could afford a real one. When Hind, Nihal, and I weren't taking turns suffocating in the back room (once Sports Palace's sauna), adding prices and security tags to books, we were on the shop floor supervising our staff, ensuring that displays were inviting, and trying to keep little nuisances from becoming larger troubles. I think most of our customers appreciated our visibility, that we weren't hiding behind closed doors. But some, accustomed to being ignored in bookstores, misinterpreted the behavior of our eager staff. Overzealous patrons insisted on returning books to shelves, often putting them in the wrong location. When our booksellers asked these patrons to let us do the reshelving, they felt they weren't trusted to do it correctly, or that we were needlessly suspicious. Sitting in the café allowed me to watch these interactions (that is, until I discovered the joy of webcams and motion sensors) and, sometimes, to address misunderstandings before they escalated. And then there was the trouble that came in through the front door: bill collectors who erroneously claimed to have come many times, in order to fine us; or a customer who had called in a favor from a police connection and filed a fabricated complaint of some wrongdoing because he hadn't been allowed to return a book. We regrouped at our table intermittently to have coffee, conduct meetings, and answer emails. Whenever my mother felt she hadn't heard sufficient news of her daughters, she would drop in to the café, knowing she would find either of the two she'd raised, or her chosen daughter, Nihal.

With time, hard work—so much hard work that in hindsight I can't fathom how we mustered the energy to sustain it—and increased book sales, the situation began to shift in our shop, and outside of it. So much happened so quickly. Diwan's second year was the start of my thirtieth. For the first time in my life, seven years into our marriage, I suggested to Number One that we have a child. He accepted. Zein was born in 2004 and Layla in 2006, just before Diwan's fourth birthday. Hind gave birth to her son, Ramzi, named after our father, in 2005. I don't know how we managed it all. It was constantly trying; I felt pulled in opposite directions.

There were small joys, and places we found relief. Eventually, we were able to afford separate office space and hire dedicated staff for the infinite tasks that we'd initially split on an ad hoc basis. An apartment became vacant on the ground floor of one of the Baehler Mansions. Miraculously (since licensing was a nightmare), it was already licensed to function as an office space. The entrance was in the courtyard, behind the main road. To one side was a wooden bench where the building's porters held court, observing and commenting on visitor comings and goings. These busybodies played versatile roles: amenable security guards, handymen, personal shoppers, and, at times, real estate agents. We'd heard about the office space from the head porter, 'Am Ibrahim, with whom I exchanged salutations every morning. He

spoke in a choppy Nubian dialect. I never understood much
of what he said, but we conversed in smiles and laughter. At
the end of every month, he would enter Diwan in his immac-
ulate white galabeya and white skullcap to collect the rent
for the owner of the building. When we moved to the new
office, he rerouted to visit us. When he died, his son took
over his duties. In our world, professions were passed on,
and people knew you even if they didn't know your name.
Relationships governed our actions far more than established
systems or written laws.

We hired a man named Mohyy as a *mukhalasati* (a finisher
or handler), a position that lacks an American counterpart.
He began as an office cleaner. He served refreshments to
visitors, ran errands, paid bills, and submitted papers at government offices. His levity was a useful counterpoint to the
debilitating bureaucracy. Everyone, from other shop workers to government officials, took a liking to him instantly.
He nurtured these relationships, exchanging phone numbers and thoughtful tokens of appreciation, so that he
could one day call in favors. As an underdog, he understood
the power of reciprocity. He avoided managers and department heads, knowing that others, at the bottom of the ladder,
did the real work.

As with all things Diwanian, our new office was uncon-
ventional: a large high-ceilinged room, which contained
three desks for the three managing partners, Hind, Nihal,
and me. One side of the room held a large bookcase, home
to signed texts by Diwan's favorite authors, upcoming releases, toys for when our children came to visit, and piles
of book catalogs. Framed newspaper clippings and photographs of business milestones—articles in the Egyptian
papers about our bestseller lists, small write-ups in foreign
publications like *Monocle*, images from the Zamalek shop's

opening—hung on the walls. Behind my desk was a bulletin board that reminded me to shoot for the stars and be myself, a picture of my daughters and me, and worn remnants of to-do lists. A receipt from the largest transaction carried out by a customer-service staff member—one and a half meters of books, worth fourteen thousand Egyptian pounds—dangled to the floor.

In the center of the room, there was a round meeting table that, at lunchtime, became a buffet: we would each unpack cutlery, crockery, and a dish from home, and share our meals with employees or visitors. In our early days, Nihal would bake chocolate cake and chocolate chip cookies at home and bring them to sell at Diwan's café. As demand increased, Nihal's workload became unmanageable, and she sought to outsource the baking. Some of the women who frequented the café expressed interest in the job. They were tested on their abilities to bake and price goods. Miriam, one of these women, ended up being our principal baked-goods supplier for over a decade, becoming known as the "cake lady." She was, I later learned, a mother of four, using her new income to fund her children's education. As Diwan grew, so did Miriam's enterprise. She went from baking at home to starting her own company that also catered to other businesses.

In our office, we overshared our problems, we overheard one another on the phone, and we made room for each other. Our accountant saw us as three ladies with a strained relationship to numbers and encouraged us to hire a midlevel accountant named Maged, whose office we placed at the other end of our headquarters. While store staff were mostly men, we primarily hired women for the new office. They shared our responsibilities for marketing, human resources, events, data, and warehousing. Maged joined Amir, Hind's Arabic-book-buying assistant, as one of the few men in the office. After handling the accounts for nine months, Maged suggested that he take the more prestigious title of finance manager. As a man looking to move up in the world, he said, he believed that titles mattered just as much as numbers. We didn't care what he called himself, as long as he eased Diwan's growing pains. He insisted on being given a large office, which he refused to share, citing the "sensitive nature" of his work. Over two decades, numerous economic crashes, devaluations, and revolutions, the size of our headquarters shrank to accommodate financial strain—that is, except for Maged's office.

Minou hated office meetings as much as she loved Diwan's decaf coffee. Whenever we needed to meet, we would do so in the café. She also wanted to see her work live, to watch people's interactions with what she had created. Diwan's logo had been her triumph, followed by Diwan's shopping bag, free with every purchase, an accidental marketing success. Right before we were due to open, with barely any start-up money left, Minou showed me her designs for beautifully crafted bags. They featured our bold logo, contrasted with a multilayered background of typography and modernized Arabo-Islamic patterns in earth tones. Coated paper. German-imported glue. Sturdy black handles. No expense spared. She'd successfully captured my attention. I asked for an initial run of ten thousand. Hind and Nihal gawked. We didn't have ten thousand books in stock! How long would it take to use the bags? Where would we store them? And how would we pay for them? My guilt was apparent enough that they refrained from telling me off further. It was the best mistake of my life. We set a trend of below-the-line advertising, which was unprecedented in our market: we never paid for advertising in a magazine or on a billboard, trusting the bags to speak for us. Whenever our stock ran low, Minou and I would meet to discuss whether to reprint or produce a different style.

"You know, koskosita"—in truth, what we called each other was way worse—"I am the artist and you are the bookseller," Minou would say before I could finish a sentence.

"So, I can't have an opinion?"

"I create. You pimp. You peddle other people's shit and take your cut. I can't believe some of the crap you sell."

"That crap pays the bills. Schopenhauer doesn't."

"Fine. Sell the lowbrow shit in plastic. Don't put it in my bags." She said all of this while smiling.

I feigned shock. "What happened to 'the customer is always right'?"

"You don't pay me enough for cunnilingus," she snapped back.

"I'm glad your corporates do, so that you keep Diwan as a passion project."

"Everyone needs a piece on the side." Patrons at nearby tables glared at us with disapproval, disturbed by what they overheard. And new staff members were terrified. When Minou hired an office manager and I finally took on a marketing manager, I could tell they dreaded the day they would have to deal with one of us alone. We cherished the verbal abuse we hurled at one another, recognizing it for what it was: a precious source of creativity and play. With every new initiative or anniversary we would meet in the café, trade foul remarks and ideas, and produce a new line of bags, each a work of art. But Minou had her rules.

"Don't send in the white witch. I can't work with her." Minou's tone shifted from threatening to wary.

"You mean Nihal? Seriously? What the fuck is wrong with you?" I said, my impatience growing.

"I can't deal with her. She's too nice. She puts those fucking homeopathy drops in my water, she disarms me, and then she screws me with her shrewdness. You never see it coming. That's her strength."

"Okay, what about Hind?"

"Definitely not. I am not fooled by her quietness. That one works from the shadows. The monochrome clothes, the flat shoes, the way she tries to go unnoticed. *Your* weapon is your noise. Hers is her silence. She scares me more. You want your fucking bags, you play by my rules, bitch." And I did. Because I wasn't the only one who wanted them. Customers had literally begun collecting them.

In 2007, for Diwan's fifth anniversary, we launched a new line of bags featuring the Hand of Fatima—the so-called five of fives, a palm-shaped symbol said to ward off evil—in deep turquoise tones. We approached the Museum of Modern Egyptian Art, housed in the grounds of the Cairo Opera House complex, with a request to host our anniversary celebration there. Our store couldn't accommodate a fraction of the friends and fans Diwan had amassed over our first half decade. They declined; museums weren't spaces for parties, and it would be disrespectful to the art to treat it as a backdrop. Instead, we compromised and celebrated in the main open-air auditorium outside the Cairo Opera House, which was separated from the Museum of Modern Egyptian Art by a courtyard with a fountain. Customers and friends filled the space, some seated in chairs, others on the ground or leaning against the surrounding arches. I remember looking up at the sky in gratitude to all the forces that had made the last five years possible. We invited five of Diwan's favorite authors—Robert Fisk, Bahaa Taher, Ahdaf Soueif, Galal Amin, and Ahmed Al-'Aidy—to talk about the past five years and the coming five. Nobody dared to hope for, or predict, the impending revolution. Ahmed, a rising young author whom Hind had selected to join the more established writers, reminisced about how, when Diwan first opened, he used to look up at the bestseller lists papering the walls and imagine his book among them. I remembered the missing ISBNs that would have threatened the existence of those lists, had Hind not soldiered on.

Diwan's café was supposed to be a quaint, idyllic haven at the heart of our bookstore. It had a mind of its own, as did its patrons. We'd made Sports Palace into a room of our own. We'd outgrown the café and rented the new office. We'd even begun to discuss expanding to a second location. There had been few spaces that welcomed women, let alone allowed them to pee, and so we'd tried to make room. As Mrs. Diwan, I tried to reimagine the role of Egyptian womanhood to fit myself and others like me. When a friend wrote on Facebook that she was "proud to be Mrs. So-and-So," I realized that I could never feel that proud of a husband, proud enough to sacrifice my identity. But I would, happily, for Diwan. The English writer Jeanette Winterson writes: "It seems to me that being the right size for your world—and knowing that both you and your world are not by any means fixed dimensions—is a valuable clue to learning how to live." I kept her guidance in mind. I built unexpected alliances and learned to compromise: with itinerant strangers, callous coworkers, and, eventually, myself. I tried to live in the spaces that let me in, or forge new ones. We all do.

"This is my daily outing. I absolutely love Diwan," said one of the café regulars with rabid enthusiasm.

"You must be a voracious reader," Nihal said admiringly.

"I come for the carrot cake."

"Good for you!" Nihal was relentless in her optimism.

2

EGYPT ESSENTIALS

We knew from the beginning that Diwan would sell books in Arabic, English, French, and German. We also knew that these categories were porous—so, early on, we decided to create a section that we called "Egypt Essentials," to house all four languages and cut across genres. Like authors of science-fiction novels, we crafted a world that existed only in our imagination. On its shelves, we wove a modern mythology using the threads of fiction, biography, history, economics, and photography. Some of the titles we chose to include became steadfast members, while others enjoyed a brief stint before returning to their permanent shelves. The section name made me think of essential oils: sold in curved glass bottles in bazaars, their origins entrenched in a secret and distant past, they distilled the intangible into a drop, a scent. Egypt Essentials promised similar access to readers, who were a mix of tourists, outsiders yearning to become insiders, and Egyptians who'd seen their country only through a keyhole.

There was a reason our section name was plural. Any singular narrative of Egypt is a lie. The story of Cairo is, primarily, a tale of two cities: one takes place in Egyptian pounds, the other in foreign currency (as the economist Galal Amin has noted). People who live on the Egyptian pound go to government schools, take public transport, and try to stay above the poverty line. Their most prized possession is a subsidy card that enables them to buy produce from government-run outlets. The size and price of one loaf of *baladi* bread governs their existence. Books are not a necessity, but a luxury. Others, like me, who exist in the sheltered, U.S.-dollar-denominated Cairo, go to international schools, often learn to speak English or French better than Arabic, shop at supermarkets and malls, have access to imported food and medicine, and employ others to cook, clean, and drive for them. Cairo is the place in which they live, but her soul does not always dwell in theirs; they have to really look to see their own city.

Hind and I competed along these lines—her Arabic books on one side, my English books on the other. While the English-language books I sourced contributed more to Diwan's bottom line, because they were bought in foreign currency and converted against an exchange rate that made them more expensive than locally produced books, Hind's Arabic books outsold mine in quantity. She never missed an opportunity to remind me of this fact, like during every monthly staff meeting. I knew that her books garnered Diwan the regional admiration and the legitimacy of a local Egyptian bookstore, setting us apart from the flimsy franchises of international bookstores that had recently begun spreading through the Gulf states.

Our ancient sibling rivalry lived on. We argued constantly. Hind was strategic: she saw the bigger picture. I, on the other hand, had hardly any impulse control, and I relished getting lost in any and all minutiae. We guarded our competing sections like military men. We fought over shelf allocations, which of our sections had higher book turnover, and the space new releases would occupy in window displays. As a kid, I'd felt endless awe and admiration for Hind, so I did what any younger sister would—I relentlessly stalked and annoyed her. When we were teenagers, our fury was mutual, as was our desire for destruction. Doors were slammed amid vows of exclusion and execution. Finally, we'd learned the value of sisterhood in a stubbornly misogynistic landscape. We became friends, vowing to support and protect one another. And through it all, we knew how to piss each other off better than anyone.

In school, we'd learned more about the exploits of William the Conqueror and Oliver Cromwell, Lord Protector of the Commonwealth, than we had of Muhammad Ali or Nasser. We encountered the ancient Egyptians alongside the Romans and the Greeks, but our country was largely absent from our contemporary lessons, save one module on the Arab-Israeli conflict. I read Shakespeare and other mainstays of the English canon before I'd heard of Imru' al-Qais or Al-Khansa'. Poorly funded state-run schools offered a "free" education in Arabic, but those who could afford to placed their children in foreign-language schools, the thriving remains of colonial, missionary, and diplomatic endeavors. Hind and I attended the British International School in Cairo, but we were very much outside of Cairo. Our weekends were Saturdays and Sundays, whereas Egypt's weekends were Fridays and Saturdays. We were not allowed to utter a word of Arabic on school premises. This was Great Britain, complete with lemon-and-sugar pancakes on Shrove Tuesday, Guy Fawkes celebrations, and charity garden fêtes. White teachers were paid in British pounds. One of these teachers who remains singed in my memory is Mr. Powell, my Junior Four teacher. He had an angry red face, stingy blue eyes, ferocious teeth, and a mouth whose corners appeared to be pulled downward. He used to hold his hand across his belly in a Napoleonic pose, and he always smelled of stale booze. "Are you deaf, daft, or stupid?" was his refrain of choice.

Like many Egyptians who went to foreign-language schools, Hind and I learned and read in a language other than Arabic. Complicated and inaccessible, classical Arabic left us linguistically orphaned; English adopted us, and we accepted all too gladly. My parents insisted we speak and write the three languages of Egypt's more recent colonial history: Arabic, English, and French. Aware of the advantages of learning the English language—which they both did in adulthood—my parents were nonetheless unwilling to sacrifice their mother tongue or sentence their daughters to a life of linguistic migration. When I was ten years old, they enlisted the help of Abla Nabeeha, a retired Arabic teacher in her seventies, who once a week attempted to instill in us the values of classical Arabic grammar. I saw this as an opportunity to consume more chocolate sables from Simonds, the timeless patisserie on 26th of July Street, which my mother brought in with tea within ten minutes of the tutor's arrival. Abla Nabeeha smelled of patience and medicine. Her heavy breasts drooped down onto an equally generous belly, which gave way to large hips. Her calves and ankles were always swollen. When she sat in the chair adjacent to mine, I noticed the tops of her socks drawing a deep indentation across her knees. She was kind to me; Arabic was not.

Fus'ha, classical Arabic, is written but seldom spoken. It is dead, what Toni Morrison calls an "unyielding language content to admire its own paralysis." It is riddled with rules that cover all grammatical formulations and leave little room for playfulness or mistakes. Hind, charmed by words and their usages, urged me to pursue the beauty beneath the rules; I couldn't see beyond the constraints. Fus'ha is the mother of all Arabic dialects, bringing forth a progeny so varied across the Arab world that different regions struggle to understand dialects other than their own. 'Amiyya, vernacular or colloquial Arabic, the bastard child of Fus'ha, is the exception. It's the language of Egypt's monumental film industry, and the reason for Egyptian Arabic's popularity throughout the region. Despite the widespread use of 'Amiyya on-screen and in life, until recently, most books were written in Fus'ha. Egyptians were torn between both languages. Readers fell through the cracks.

As young adults, Hind and I, natives who had a complicated relationship with our mother tongue, had become aware of our dislocation from our motherland. With our newfound freedom, we spent our university years in search of our country and ourselves. Hind studied political science and read Arabic literature for fun. I studied English and comparative literature. Outside class, we discovered unfamiliar parts of the city brimming with new life—repurposed buildings and alleyways, flea markets, used-book markets, music festivals, and fringe theater. Our search for a deeper sense of origin, and what we encountered en route, would be integral to Diwan. It quickly became apparent that many of Diwan's readers were similarly dislocated from their roots and lost in linguistic migration. We didn't want to punish them; we wanted to invite them in.

Egypt Essentials began with the obvious: books about ancient Egypt, from coffee-table books, to mini guidebooks covering specific monuments or areas, to fiction. Wilbur Smith, the Zambian author, took center stage. His sales worldwide were eclipsed by mystery and thriller writers like

John Grisham and Stephen King, but in Diwan, he had a devout following of ancient-Egyptophiles. His book covers bear images of pyramids, camels, and sunsets. Kings and kingdoms are narrated through the eyes of Taita, a clever and ambitious eunuch, ex-slave, general, and adviser to the pharaoh. Before this, my knowledge of my ancestors had been limited to broad strokes: seven millennia, a handful of gods, leading characters like Ramesses II, Hatshepsut, and the trinity of Osiris, Isis, and Horus, accompanied by temples, scribes, and hieroglyphics. I knew the importance of death and the afterlife. I had no knowledge of how my ancestors lived, baked, farmed, or loved.

Both masters and beneficiaries of cultural colonialism, the French have their own ancient-Egyptophile: Christian Jacq, a bestselling author and Egyptologist. Diwan's readers of English and French literature gorged themselves on his books. In my attempt to understand our customers, I read through one of his most popular series, The Stone of Light, which takes place in Upper Egypt on the west bank of the Nile River, home to the artisans working on tombs in the nearby Valley of the Kings. I was struck by his level of detail, which distinguishes his writing from his less academic counterparts, as he weaves real figures and historical events into his fictional worlds.

My reliance upon a Frenchman to elucidate my own history underlines an uncomfortable fact: with some exceptions, Egyptians seldom write novels set in ancient Egypt. There's a double irony in the way that colonialism first severs us from our past and then forces us to turn to the colonizers for knowledge of that very past. Westerners created Egyptology, then taught it to the Egyptians. It's like the Antiquities Service, a government program started in mid-nineteenth-century Egypt ostensibly to control the trade of Egyptian artifacts. It actually acted as an extension of neocolonialism: the program was headed by French scholars, and most Egyptian archaeologists weren't even granted permission to excavate in their own country. An Egyptian wasn't appointed to run the program until the 1950s. As an adult, I finally saw the bust of Nefertiti—at the Neues Museum in Berlin. The British Museum has the Rosetta Stone (and over fifty thousand other ancient Egyptian objects, making it the largest collection outside of Egypt) and still refuses to repatriate it. Bastards.

The more I think about it, the more I wonder how our reliance on imported knowledge limits our ability to imagine. Are colonized cultures so accustomed to being othered that we unquestioningly accept that knowledge as a gift, never thinking of veracity or reciprocity? Eastern writers don't narrate Western experience as much as Western writers narrate Eastern experience. Who owns the past: the creators of its narratives, or their consumers? Is it writers or readers who are responsible for filling in the gaps left by colonial estrangement?

"I can't find Christian Jacq's *Champollion l'égyptien*," Dr. Medhat, a distinguished ginger-haired, blue-eyed older gentleman, and one of my regulars, said one afternoon. "Do you have it in stock? It's not on the shelves." He removed his brown horn-rimmed glasses, befuddled. His desperation reminded me of when my twelve-year-old self would finish one Agatha Christie mystery and urgently seek out the next one. I walked toward the computer terminal near the café, knowing that to double-check the shelves would be taken as a slight by Dr. Medhat.

He followed me, saying, "You should read these books." I stared intently into the screen. He mistook my silence for interest. "Getting to know ancient Egypt teaches me so much about our Egypt today. Did you know that the term 'reinvent the wheel' refers to us?" I gave him an incredulous look, as he continued with glee. "Yes, they invented the wheel in one dynasty, then the technology was lost over time, and they ended up reinventing it centuries later." His charming anecdote went against my (admittedly limited) knowledge.

"Doesn't that seem a little out of character? The ancient Egyptians were manic about writing things down. Look at the magic spells, wills, medical procedures, and tax records that scribes documented; we take after them in our love for minutiae and bureaucracy," I replied.

"You have a point, but of the wheel issue, I'm certain." His hands descended deeper into his pockets, as if anchoring himself into the ground. He looked around, his eyes landing on a nearby table of new releases, including Alaa Al-Aswany's collection of Arabic short stories *Friendly Fire*. Its prominent cover, depicting a row of ancient Egyptian figures facing a can of Flit insecticide, elicited Dr. Medhat's less friendly fire. "What impudence! How dare he insult our glorious past? Our fall from grandeur to decadence, c'est trop!" He paced around the table, flustered.

"I don't think Dr. Aswany means any harm. He's merely suggesting that we stop basking in our glorious past and focus on improving our present. We've become victims of our pyramid schemes: we swallow the feel-good pill of 'we built the pyramids' while our house crumbles around us." I flashed him my most engaging grin. My father taught me that I could get away with saying anything to anyone, as long as I did it with a smile. "Is it acceptable that the descendants of the people who built the pyramids are now living in redbrick monstrosities?"

"But even Plato believed that when compared to the Egyptians, the Greeks were nothing more than childish mathematicians," he proclaimed with renewed fervor.

"It's good to see you, Dr. Medhat. Customer services will call you as soon as *Champollion l'égyptien* arrives," I concluded with another smile.

The conversation stuck with me. His patriotism, and his reading habits, seemed to further derail him from the very knowledge he sought out. Or maybe it was his disappointment with the last fifty years of government failure. But history is a living thing, subject to interpretation. And so is literature. Knowing why we read, what urges it satisfies—to escape, to connect with a past that was concealed from us, to rekindle nationalist pride—may help. But perhaps questioning *how* we read is more important. Insight rises out of discomfort, and I doubted Dr. Medhat's capacity for discomfort.

As we continued to develop Egypt Essentials, we stocked books covering the saints, monasteries, art, and civilization of the Coptic period. Spanning from the third to the seventh centuries, this period witnessed the cultural shift from ancient Egyptian religious practices to Coptic Christianity, a movement whose contemporary followers constitute the largest Christian population in the country. Still, the books elicited some distasteful comments.

"Customers complain that we have too many books about Copts, and not enough about Muslims," said Hossam, one of my least favorite customer-service employees, a characteristic blob of saliva trapped in the corner of his mouth.

"Whether these are the opinions of customers, or just yours, we are each entitled to our own. Here's mine: 'Too many' as opposed to what? Christianity came to Egypt in AD 33. The word 'Copt' comes from the word for 'Egyptian' in Greek. The ancient Egyptians were conquered by the Hyksos, Nubians, Assyrians, Libyans, Persians, Greeks, and Romans. The Copts are probably their closest descendants. As for the Muslims, remind me again, when did Islam make it to our part of the world?" I walked away to cool off.

There was so much more that I wanted to say to Hossam, but I'd had this discussion enough times to know that arguing wouldn't help. Though his remark may seem innocuous, it reveals a gap in our cultural understanding: a craving for Islamic hegemony that engenders a complete denial of difference, and of history itself. The Islamic conquest of Roman Egypt occurred around AD 640 under the military leader 'Amr ibn Al-'As. After a few years of sieges and battles, Egypt fell, and gradual, state-sanctioned Islamization began. First came the *gizya*, a heavy tax levied on those who refused to convert to Islam. Language followed: Arabic replaced Coptic and Greek (the languages of the Greek and Roman occupations of Egypt) as the dominant vernacular, then it became the language of the nation by law. In 1919, Egyptian revolutionaries used the symbols of the crescent and the cross in the streets to signify unity against British colonial occupation. From 1923 to 1953, Egypt's flag was a crescent with three five-pointed stars. The crescent was said to symbolize Islam; the three stars were interpreted as either the three lands of Egypt, Nubia, and Sudan, or the three faiths of Islam, Christianity, and Judaism, peacefully coexisting. Still, people like Hossam were threatened by minority non-Muslim denominations, even though one in every ten Egyptians is a Copt.

The tension strikes a personal chord. I grew up with the promise of solidarity and unity. My mother was Coptic and my father was Muslim. They narrated history as a long arc, teaching Arabic, French, and English not as inherently dominant languages but as recent manifestations of a long series of conquests of Egypt spanning millennia. It wasn't personal, just colonial. But in recent decades, acceptance of otherness and tolerance of religious difference seem to have faded. I wonder if tolerance is learned, like reading—a habit ingrained in Hind and me from a young age. Perhaps others lack the privilege.

Cairo's and Alexandria's cosmopolitan histories, the indispensable influence of its Greek, Armenian, Italian, and French populations, came to life in Egypt Essentials. Lucette Lagnado's *The Man in the White Sharkskin Suit* tells the tale of her Jewish family and their exodus from Egypt as a result of Nasser's post-1956 purges of foreigners. Colette Rossant's *Apricots on the Nile: A Memoir with Recipes* captures her upbringing in an Egyptian Jewish family during Cairo's war years. In her portrait of 1930s and '40s Egypt, *Oleander, Jacaranda,* Penelope Lively narrates her experiences of Cairo life through the eyes of the colonizer's child. As a British girl, she admires the freedom of barefoot peasant children, the significance of their poverty lost on her. These knotty memoirs are reflective without succumbing to nostalgia. They multiply, and complicate, stories of nationhood. I hoped the wide range of voices would shift (even slightly) the mindsets of readers like Hossam by encouraging them to sit in discomfort and listen.

And when we did Islam, we did it Diwan-style. We rejected religious polemics. We did not stock texts about *ahadith*, sayings of the Prophet, or the different schools of Islamic jurisprudence that besieged existing bookstores. Instead, we sold books about *mulids*, festivals celebrating the births of saints, Sufism, poetry, calligraphy, architecture, and the artistry of woodwork, carpets, and pottery. We challenged ourselves and others to read history as a changing entity, rather than a lifeless, linear record. We presented and lobbied for a study in fragments of a history in fragments.

Then, we plucked from gardens farther away: books of Egyptian proverbs whose titles were quirky literal English translations of popular idioms: *The Son of a Duck Is a Floater. Unload Your Own Donkey. Apricots Tomorrow.* There was a disarming simplicity in their delivery of tried-and-true outcomes. The collected sayings were a kind of popular archive, carrying wisdom across generations. Written and spoken in the colloquial Arabic of the masses and then translated into English, the sayings in these volumes were accessible to a broad spectrum of readers. But as literal translations, without cultural context, they were charmingly nonsensical. Crossing between languages gave them a grittiness and friction. Their texture transcended the axiomatic, becoming a sort of truth in itself.

As Hind, Nihal, and I considered the section we'd created, we knew it wasn't complete without the works of Naguib Mahfouz, Egypt's Nobel laureate and the author of *The Cairo Trilogy*. When Mahfouz's novels arrived in the store, Ahmed, a born salesman and my favorite bookseller, with his tidy appearance, engaging smile, and quick learning, arranged them in alphabetical order. I walked up behind him, surveying his work. Without turning, as if addressing the shelves, he asked me why Youssef Idris wasn't included in the section.

"Personally, Ahmed, he is one of my favorite authors. He was one of the four Arab contenders for the Nobel Prize, but he didn't get it."

"Why?"

"Denys Johnson-Davies, the leading translator of Arabic literature at the time, said that he wasn't translated widely enough into French and English; others said that he was a master of the short story, and the Swedes preferred novels."

"That's not fair."

"My aunt makes the best basboussa in the world, but Tseppas has a chain of shops where they sell their soulless version. It's not about fairness, it's about reach." Ahmed nodded in acknowledgment, knowing our conversation was over. (In truth, my aunt's basboussa sucked. I'd borrowed the analogy from Ziad, one of our five business partners, who'd used it many times to shut me up. Ziad is notable for many reasons, including the fact that he's the only person I've ever met who's never once uttered a swear word. I made a bet with Hind that one day his decorum will fracture and he'll release a filthy torrent of invective. Luckily for me, the bet doesn't have a deadline.)

Translation is essential. Access to translated literature nourishes and affirms the imagination. It's perhaps even more important to authors writing in languages other than English who hope to enter the mainstream, like Youssef Idris and Naguib Mahfouz. Denys Johnson-Davies was credited with saving Alifa Rifaat's short stories from the ashes of perdition. I've witnessed too many books poorly translated and thus condemned to linguistic purgatory.

Ahmed's question about Youssef's absence helped to clarify the format of Egypt Essentials. It must be fluid. I envisioned it as an extension of my own family's habits. Ours is an open house: family members congregate every Friday for lunch, and we invite friends to join as guests at our table on a revolving basis. I reminded myself that the section, and Diwan itself, couldn't encompass all that's been written about Egypt. We were cubists, offering varied perspectives and angles from which to view the same subject. These books gave readers the chance to create their own literary experiences: the meeting of the writer, the reader, and the historical moment when the act of reading takes place. No two readers will ever read the same book in the same way.

For an economic perspective, we ordered Galal Amin's Arabic bestseller, and its English translation, *Whatever Happened to the Egyptians?* I'd known Dr. Galal when I was a student at the American University in Cairo, where I attended his lectures. I can vividly recall his robust, jovial figure standing at the podium, his sky-high hair and his observant eyes. As students asked questions, he'd rest his fingers in a circle on his forehead. He'd explain our nation's recent history, how mightily we'd fallen from our ancient status as builders of pyramids and inventors of mathematics, irrigation, and astronomy, intermittently chuckling as he spoke. The more provocative his answer, the greater his mirth. He followed the wild success of his first book with an additional account: *Whatever Else Happened to the Egyptians?*

Dr. Galal—I could never bring myself to omit his title, even after graduating—spoke of an Egypt on the brink of attrition. Through eclectic histories, including of the television, the telephone, romance, birthdays, the circus, and the train, he examined a country shaped by socioeconomic forces. When he visited Diwan well after the 2011 revolution,

I suggested a title for another book in the series. He leaned in inquisitively, tilting his ear toward me. I whispered, *"What the Fuck Else Can Happen to the Egyptians?"* He threw his head back in a guffaw. That was our last interaction; he died in September 2018.

In "This World and the Next," the last chapter of the second book in the series, he quotes from a speech his father, a notable academic, gave when he was a schoolboy, about how religion enforces a culture of resignation, precluding political and social progress by encouraging us to take comfort in the afterlife. Does the ancient Egyptian obsession with death come from a similar dynamic? Our ancestors built pyramids to house and honor their deceased. They wrote *The Egyptian Book of the Dead* (a generic name for manuals of spells said to help souls navigate the afterlife). Contemporary Egyptians don't have the same level of interest or comfort in writing or reading about death, although the way both Muslims and Christians handle death originates from the rituals of ancient Egyptians. The forty-day timeline recurs. For my ancestors, this was the time allotted to the first phase of mummification (dehydration). For Muslims and Copts today, forty days marks the mourning period, during which close female relatives wear black. On the fortieth day, they hold a day of mourning and remembrance. In the seventeenth century, forty days—the etymology of the word "quarantine"—was the period of time a ship suspected of carrying disease or plague was kept in isolation.

A few shelves below Dr. Galal, browsing visitors would find Agatha Christie's *Death on the Nile*, an iconic murder mystery set in the 1930s between Cairo and Upper Egypt. Hercule Poirot, the Belgian detective, finds himself on a luxurious

Nile cruise with a curious cast of characters. One of them, an American heiress, is murdered. Poirot and his sidekick, Colonel Race, investigate their fellow travelers, every one of whom seems to have sufficient motive. It joined the category of Egypt Essentials as a visitor, not a family member. Mystery, like fantasy and science fiction, got little traction in the early 2000s with Arab readers, unlike the more popular genres: literary fiction, history and politics, biography, and poetry. *Death on the Nile* was the exception. It reeled in Diwan's customers, nostalgic for the exotic 1930s Egypt of their parents' and grandparents' stories.

Nostalgia, a permanent resident in the hearts of so many Egyptians, sells books. Minou always chided me about the books we sold in her bags. The bodice rippers, whose damsels in distress needed to be saved by chiseled heroes. The self-help manuals. The dating guides. Any books, really, that ignored the violence of white men. Of course she disapproved of the photographic books that gazed longingly at Egypt's landscape, as colonizers once had. As usual, I ignored her. I stocked Alain Blottière's *Vintage Egypt: Cruising the Nile in the Golden Age of Travel* and Andrew Humphreys's *Grand Hotels of Egypt* and its follow-up, *On the Nile in the Golden Age of Travel* in Egypt Essentials, because I knew they'd sell. These collections cataloged the storied visitors of yore who'd traveled to Egypt in the late nineteenth and early twentieth centuries, such as Amelia Edwards, Rudyard Kipling, Florence Nightingale, Arthur Conan Doyle, Jean Cocteau—what they did and where they stayed. Thousands of foreigners packed their fantasies and set sail for Egypt's shores every year, intermingling with the already Westernized Egyptian upper class and the Europeans who had made Cairo and Alexandria home. Shops and restaurants opened to cater to their opulent tastes. They took photographs, too:

riding camels through the desert, racing in a Bugatti at the foot of the pyramids, sipping tea at the Mena House Hotel, and cruising down the Nile on a steam *dahabeya*.

As a young teenager, I borrowed Agatha Christie's novels from the All Saints Cathedral lending library. When I realized that she had died a decade beforehand, I was suddenly overwhelmed with grief for the mortal lives of writers. I resolved to read everything she had ever written. This incited my lifelong habit of hoarding books and building libraries. And *Death on the Nile* remains my favorite of hers. As an Egyptian in a school that was unapologetic in its British supremacy, I felt proud that Agatha had deemed Upper Egypt a worthy setting. I was twelve years old. Chimamanda Ngozi Adichie was only nine, and, I would later learn, still writing stories in which white characters ate apples, drank ginger beer, and played in the snow—all elements from the English-language stories she read, all absent from her Nigerian reality. Decades later, I heard her speak about "the danger of a single story" with intimate recognition. Being educated outside of my mother tongue led me to believe that Egypt, and Egyptians, couldn't exist in white people's literature, because their literature did not belong to us, and ours used to be of no interest to them.

Tourists shopping at Diwan purchased a copy of *Death on the Nile*, and often excitedly shared their plans for embarking on a Nile cruise. They would sit on the veranda of the Cataract Hotel, posing as Hercule Poirot and Colonel Race. They would walk past the suite Agatha once stayed in, which carries her name. I smiled at the quaint reenactments these tourists performed. As children, Hind and I had accompanied our mother on the same mission to Aswan, a prominent city on the southern part of the Nile River. She wanted to acquaint us with our ancient past, to share an intimate experience, and to instill pride in our collective legacy. Later, I took my daughters, Zein, then ten, and Layla, eight, on the same trip. We sat in the shade of the Cataract Hotel's veranda, as Agatha, her sleuths, and countless tourists had, watching the sun's glow on the Nile. I explained that the ancient Egyptians worshipped the sun as a trinity: heat, rays, and essence. Nodding, my daughters sipped their lemonades. I picked up my bottle of Sakara Gold, printed with the image of the step pyramid of Saqqara, refilling my glass.

Finally, I suggested we watch the film adaptation of *Death on the Nile*. I'd first seen it in the mid-1980s on our new VHS player. I remembered the cardboard cover of the tape showing Peter Ustinov as Poirot, staring out into the horizon, framed by the imposing figure of the Sphinx. The background was Hollywood's reductive take on the essence of Egypt: a pyramid, feluccas adrift on the Nile, and the paddle steamer SS *Memnon* (built for Thomas Cook in 1904). The faces of the cast perforated the border of the image: Bette Davis, Mia Farrow, Angela Lansbury, David Niven, Maggie Smith, Sam Wanamaker. They came to Egypt, stayed at the Cataract, and filmed at the Giza pyramids and in Luxor's temples. My daughters had never heard of any of these Hollywood stars. That familiar childhood uncertainty of my culture's worthiness rose from deep inside me, this time in defense of the Hollywood greats I had watched with my parents. I pulled out my phone and looked up the movie, trying to find a hook that would capture their attention.

"Wayne Sleep choreographed the tango," I announced with excitement.

"What's a tango?" asked an uninterested Zein.

"Who's Wayne Sleep?" chimed in Layla, playing along.

"They would start makeup at four a.m. to avoid filming at midday when the sun was fifty-four degrees centigrade." They were silent. "Even though this was filmed in the late 1970s, they wanted to give it a 1930s feel."

"Mom, no disrespect, but is there a more modern version? Something with Lara Croft, maybe?"

"Fuck you and fuck Lara Croft," I snapped, defeated. Maybe the internet gave them a mobility that made questions of belonging and worthiness obsolete. They were raised in a generation that wasn't forced to encounter the politics of cultural denigration and hierarchy. Theirs was a world that existed only in the present, unburdened by whatever came before. Their lives had a kind of neatness: curated, digitized, filtered.

Diwan shared my daughters' globalist upbringing. Most of the English-language books we sold traveled from distant lands, tourists who never returned to their home countries. We ordered them from the United Kingdom and the United States via an intricate web of international sales representatives, and then consolidated them in storage facilities. Once we reached cost-efficient quota, these books crossed land and water to reach either Cairo's airport or the port in Alexandria. There, they had their first encounter with red tape, pink slips, and illegible blue ink, passing through customs and censorship. Then hundreds of cardboard boxes arrived at Diwan's warehouse to be ripped open, their contents security-tagged, bar-coded, and priced. These imported titles commanded hefty prices compared to their native counterparts, Arabic books from local publishers. An average Egyptian novel was priced at 20 Egyptian pounds in the early 2000s, while *Death on the Nile* retailed for $8.99 and sold for 54 Egyptian pounds, which became a staggering 162 pounds after the devaluation of the Egyptian pound in November 2016. A mounting crescendo of emails, negotiations, and arguments over discounts, net prices, and short ships—bookseller lingo for discrepancies between packages and attached invoices—accompanied every shipment. Even more trying was the length of this cycle: from ordering to stacking, a title could take between four weeks and four months before finding itself comfortably resting on one of Diwan's shelves.

When these books finally reached their destination, I treated them with the kindness granted to weary travelers. I created intricate displays, where contrasting arrangements of books participated in lively conversation. Bookselling, too, is a dialogue, and as with every dialogue, there are people who drive it, participate in it, interrupt it, or simply eavesdrop on it. Booksellers transcend their job titles, shifting between roles to act as guardians, matchmakers, and the devisers and detectors of trends.

Perhaps reading is like traveling. We go to distant lands to understand difference. In doing so, we meet ourselves, the filter through which experience passes, as through a camera's lens. One of my favorite portraits of Egypt comes from Waguih Ghali's *Beer in the Snooker Club*. Written in English and published in 1964, the story takes place during Nasser's rule. Ram, the privileged Egyptian narrator, has just returned from England to an Egypt he struggles to understand. Ram is loosely modeled on the author himself, who died by suicide five years after the book's publication. Initially hailed as a masterpiece in the literature of emigration, the book was forgotten for decades, then republished twenty years after going out of print. Like other books in Egypt Essentials, *Beer in the Snooker Club* blurred the borders we imagine between countries. Waguih, describing his Egyptian homeland in English, feels no compulsion to explain Egypt. Instead, he speaks to an experience shared among readers: a desire to belong and a fear of leaving oneself behind.

Waguih's Egypt recalls the stories my mother told me growing up. She described afternoon teas at Groppi, Cairo's premier restaurant, tearoom, patisserie, and deli, where she and her family consumed ice cream in the summer and exquisite gateaux in the winter—the same restaurant where Waguih's narrator, Ram, meets friends for whiskey. My mother and Ram rode the same tram from Zamalek to the pyramids, the number 15 that once passed in front of the Baehler mansions on what was then Fouad I Street. She traveled within Cairo by bus or tram, and took the train to other cities. All had first- and second-class carriages. Today, public transportation is only used by those who cannot afford the necessary luxury of a car.

In our English-language sections, there were two main types of bestsellers: the current releases, carried over from *The New York Times* or London's *Sunday Times*, and the time-worn classics, most of which had some connection to Egypt, like *Death on the Nile* and *Beer in the Snooker Club*. Even my local customers bought these books, as if eager to see themselves. I get it. I feel proud of Egypt's rise to international prominence. But the pleasure is bittersweet. When your Arabic fluency has been suppressed by years of education in English and French, then a glimpse of Egypt's soul—a promise of reclamation and redemption—may be accessible only through someone else's words.

Egypt Essentials was a small section that posed a series of questions without claiming to answer them. Searching for something, I gathered images of my home in one place. Our eclectic collection introduced the colonizer to the colonized, the historians to the novelists, the locals to the outsiders. Competing realities existed side by side in competing Egypts—extreme conservatism and a liberalism devoid of roots, offensive poverty and even more offensive wealth. They always have, and they always will. In my memories, as in Cairo's streets, the present never fully overthrows the past, nor do the two coalesce. Like bickering neighbors, they delight in existing side by side in joint discord.

3

COOKERY

Though cookbooks took up only one wall in Diwan's café, they had a far greater significance in our lives than their modest display implied. To create the English cookery section (Hind presided over its Arabic counterpart), I consulted family and friends. I asked them to share their favorites: Julia Child, Mary Berry, Nigella Lawson, Jamie Oliver, Ina Garten, Madhur Jaffrey, and Ken Hom. The anomalies were *The Momo Cookbook* and the River Cafe series, which signaled the shift from individual celebrity chefs to more diffuse celebrity restaurant brands. My mother was mortified by the absence of *Larousse Gastronomique*. Though I was skeptical, I remedied the oversight, only to discover that it became a steady seller, despite its girth and stringent instructions. Once I'd struck a balance between various flavors, styles, and movements, I attempted to infuse the canonical with the local.

As I began to research Middle Eastern and Egyptian cooking, Claudia Roden emerged as queen. Born in Egypt in 1936, she launched her career with *A Book of Middle Eastern Food* and has reigned supreme ever since. The language of her titles reflected her singular command over our cuisine, from *Claudia Roden's Invitation to Mediterranean Cooking* and *Claudia Roden's Foolproof Mediterranean Cooking* to the more poetic *Tamarind and Saffron: Favorite Recipes from the*

Middle East. Though some Egyptians were happy enough to claim her as our culinary ambassador, she'd never dedicated an entire cookbook to Egyptian cooking. Instead, she blended all countries of the region into one multinational tagine.

My search for an Egyptian-specific cookbook in English yielded a single title, Samia Abdennour's 1985 *Egyptian Cooking: A Practical Guide.* Meanwhile, cooking began to inflect other genres, spilling into memoirs and biographies, beginning with Colette Rossant's *Apricots on the Nile*, in the Egypt Essentials section. I recognized the tastes and smells of the author's childhood. I craved more. In 2006, Magda Mehdawy's *My Egyptian Grandmother's Kitchen* arrived. Alongside family recipes and oral histories, she described winemaking techniques of the ancient Egyptians, offered cultural explanations and anecdotes, and set menus for specific feasts.

Celebrations are defined by what we consume in their honor. Sham el Nessim (literally "the smelling of the breeze"), observed by Egyptians since 2700 BC, marks the coming of spring. We picnic on *feseekh*, *ringa*, eggs, and spring onions. This always takes place the day after Coptic Easter, but it is observed by all Egyptians regardless of affiliation. On Eid al-Adha, Muslims honor the willingness of Abraham to sacrifice his son to obey the will of God, who provided a lamb to be slaughtered in his son's place. At dawn, following Eid prayers, lambs across Egypt are sacrificed, their meat divided into thirds: one for the family, one for friends and relatives, and one for the poor.

Though our cuisine is inextricable from our culture, I still struggled to find Egyptian cookbooks. Dissatisfied with my meager results, I asked my mother, a spectacular cook, where her culinary prowess came from.

"I used to watch your father cook. He had his specialties—leg of lamb with cinnamon and juniper, pickled cucumbers and turnips, his *fuul* with *tehina*."

"But when you first got married—"

"I just had one cookbook: Abla Nazeera. It was essential, part of every bride's trousseau, including those of my friends," she recalled. "I had one friend who used Abla Nazeera's cookbook but claimed not to. Another friend was cunning in a different way. Whenever I asked her for a recipe, she would share it in exquisite detail, but then I realized that she always withheld one essential ingredient, so no one's dishes would be as good as hers."

"Smart woman."

"Only while she had us fooled," my mother countered.

Nazeera Nicola (her surname is pronounced *Na'ula* in Arabic) was affectionately known by generations of Egyptian and Arab women as Abla ("teacher," or a respectful title for an older woman) Nazeera. Her book, *Usul al-Tahyy* (*Principles of Cooking*), was the Arab world's first encyclopedia of recipes. She studied at the Faculty of Home Economics in Cairo. In 1926, she was selected by the Ministry of Education to continue her education abroad, alongside her school's other top-performing students. Defying convention—women were expected to remain at home—Abla Nazeera's family permitted her to go to the Gloucestershire Training College of Domestic Science, in England, where she studied culinary arts and needlework for three years. When she returned to Egypt, she taught at the Saneya School for Girls, and later became an inspector general at the Ministry of Education. *Usul al-Tahyy*, her celebrated book, coauthored with Baheya

Osman, was the outcome of a competition organized by the Ministry of Education to produce an educational cookbook. Originally published in 1953, it would become the quintessential cookbook of the Arab world, with multiple editions, modernizations, and supplemental chapters featuring new recipes and styles.

Beginning in the 1940s, Abla Nazeera was a recurring voice on Egyptian radio. Between 1941 and 1952, she coauthored six textbooks on cooking and home economics. In 1973, she was honored for her work in the field of women's education, receiving a medal commemorating the opening of the first state school for girls one hundred years earlier, in 1873. By the time she passed away in 1992, at the age of ninety, she was a household icon whose influence spanned generations.

Hind stocked Abla Nazeera in her cookery section. Written in classical Arabic, the book's florid language was only lightly adorned with sparse illustrations. I scoured lists and databases for an English edition, but none existed. I asked Amir, Hind's assistant (and a future book buyer of ours), to find one for me, hoping that a local publisher had translated it. In the world of Arabic publishing in the early 2000s, databases were like genies: we'd all heard of them and we would have welcomed their presence in our lives, but we were under no illusion as to the likelihood of that happening.

"Is this book for Diwan, or for you personally?" Amir asked, puzzled.

"Both. Why?"

"I can't picture you with an apron, standing at the stove, ya Ustazah." He was right. At that point in my life, my cooking repertoire consisted of boiled and scrambled eggs, and baking was as stressful as a visit from the tax inspector.

Number One, an American, made unforgettable lasagna. When we married, his mother, a resident of South Carolina, an ardent golfer, and president of the gardening club, had given me a corrective gift: *Joy of Cooking*. I didn't know how to respond to her careful penmanship on the inside flap of the red-and-white book jacket: "The way to a man's heart is through his stomach." I didn't tell her that this was not my preferred route. Instead, I joked about her image of me as the Angel in the House: in a sweet apron, perhaps broderie anglaise or gingham, with coiffed curls. I suppressed my urge to give her an accompanying head tilt.

In 1999, three years into my marriage, Hind returned from a trip to London with a copy of a newly released cookbook by Jamie Oliver. (Little did I know then how much angst this particular chef's metaphoric nudity would cause me after we started Diwan.) Books like that one—English, nonessential, frivolous—would never have been found in Cairo's existing bookshops. Before Diwan, no one thought they had a market. And there was no market. Jamie Oliver whacked and whizzed his way into my life with his noisy shirts and schoolboy enthusiasm over a glug of balsamic vinegar and a dollop of ricotta. He discarded the exacting measurements of liters and teaspoons in favor of smidgens, bunches, and handfuls. He gave me the confidence to enter the kitchen and claim it as my own, a feat I wouldn't have dared attempt in my premarital home.

Growing up, Hind and I had a nanny named Fatma. She was diabetic, dictatorial, fiercely traditional, and kind. She lived in the neighborhood of al-Matariya, north of the well-to-do suburb of Heliopolis and south of El Marg, bordering the governorate of Qalyubia. During the day, though, our kitchen was her domain. Once, Hind and I visited her home and played football with her son on the roof of their modest apartment building. Afterward, when Fatma fed us *kofta* for lunch, I asked for ketchup, and her husband asked what that was. The roads to the house weren't paved, but they were spacious and clean—Cairo's streets hadn't yet succumbed to the disarray of overpopulation and the absence of basic government services. The discrepancies between our lifestyles were not so pronounced. Today, very few people allow their children to play with the offspring of their domestic staff. The divides have exceeded the commonalities.

As Hind and I grew older and no longer needed a nanny, Fatma became our cook, and a far more intimidating version of herself. My mother trained her in a repertoire of recipes until she was an expert. My father, on occasion, would venture into the kitchen and cook his favorites. But his more essential role lay in the procurement of ingredients. Throughout my childhood, I shopped with my parents at the different stalls on 26th of July Street. Our modest interactions with vendors and patrons deepened into lasting personal relationships. My father bought his meat from Bolbol, the butcher, who seemed related to Fares, the fishmonger, who manned the shop next to him. "Bolbol" is usually a nickname for Nabil, though I never learned his real name. He could carry conversations in French, English, German, Italian, and Spanish. It was rumored that he owned a villa in the South of France. They always greeted each other: Bolbol addressed my father as king; my father reciprocated, calling him *basha*. My father would plant himself behind the counter and sort through different cuts. He didn't mind that the cuff of his handmade shirts got soiled with blood. They discussed their meat in code. "Without any writing," my father would insist, meaning that any white tendons should be knifed out. Bolbol would give his knowing smile. As he got to work, my father would stand next to him, peering over his shoulder, overseeing the cleaning and the trimming. He was unable to delegate this particular task to my mother, who would rather call Bolbol and instruct him to deliver the cuts on her list. My father never trusted meat that he didn't select in person. He tolerated my mother ordering fruits and vegetables by phone, though he always chided her for not picking them out from the stalls. Looking back, I realize that my father was the first demanding customer I knew: the man who taught me to nudge, barter, and interrogate his vendors without degrading them.

After visiting the shops, my father would bring the goods back to Fatma, who continued to cook for our family for decades. When her husband died and her son got married, she gave him their family home and moved in with us, cementing her status as a part of our family. Her son would come to visit her, eat lunch at our kitchen table, and collect her salary. Fatma's brother was my parents' driver. Like Fatma, he was illiterate. Unlike Fatma, he smoked hashish cigarettes. When Fatma's eyes failed her, my parents suggested that 'Am Beshir, our *sofragi* (a household assistant who handles general upkeep), cook under her pedagogy.

'Am Beshir was Nubian, a short and bent man with a mizzle of hair. I remember him as old and defeated, throwing his head back to drain the last drops of booze from any glass before depositing it in the sink. He had four sons, an ailing mother who promised to leave this life but never did, a wife who bullied him, and more grandchildren than he cared to count. Fatma instructed him on the prep work of washing and chopping. My mother was fascinated by Fatma's ability to get others to do her bidding. My father loved cooking and being in the kitchen. Fatma, conscious of the source of her power, guarded the space like a fortress. My mother and 'Am Beshir, who shared a quiet resilience, did nothing until the conflict resolved itself eventually. When Fatma passed away, my father bossed around 'Am Beshir as Fatma once had. When my father died, my mother replaced him as chief order issuer. Though Hind and I were unaware of these hierarchies, we instinctively avoided the family kitchen throughout our childhood. Hind, who shared my father's love of cooking and my mother's patience and tenacity, would reenter the kitchen in her forties—as a student at Le Cordon Bleu in London.

Around the mid-2000s, family cooks and grandmothers began to be replaced by celebrity chefs, the stars of Egypt's newly hatched satellite television channels. These chefs spawned a flurry of cookbooks, written in informal Arabic, with styled photographs. In their wake, Hind's Arabic cookery section began to resemble my English one. Culinary power emanated from these famous cooks; readers trusted their qualifications without question. In their author photographs, as well as on their cooking shows, the male chefs posed in professional kitchens, donning the traditional *toque blanche* and white double-breasted jacket. The female cooks didn't wear uniforms and were often photographed with their hair done, heavily made up, with an accompanying head tilt meant to conjure domestic bliss. Interestingly, because their shows aired on satellite channels, they extended their repertoires to encompass regional dishes to cater to a wider audience, just as Claudia Roden had done decades earlier with her cookbooks.

Next, the Egyptian restaurant cookbook arrived in Cairo, and in Diwan, delayed by the centrality of the home in food culture. In 2013, a restaurant located down the block from Diwan chronicled its recipes in *Authentic Egyptian Cooking: From the Table of Abou El Sid*. The following year brought *Cairo Kitchen Cookbook: Recipes from the Middle East Inspired by the Street Food of Cairo*. These were not translated into Arabic, because their target audience was never the mainstream local book market. Still, English-speaking Egyptians bought them out of a sense of pride, or, as I believed, a mixture of nationalism and narcissism. Internationally, these cookbooks corresponded with a burgeoning trend toward "fusion," commercializing and combining local tastes for global markets.

Diwan's cookery section underlined a simple fact, gleaned over years of observing Fatma, my parents, and Hind: in Egypt, food is about much more than eating. In the kitchen of our office, clusters of staff members, depending on status and background, breakfasted together, chipping in to buy a selection of bread, cheese, olives, and fuul and *taamiya* sandwiches. They joked that *lo'ma haneya tekafi meyya*: a kind bite is enough to feed a hundred people.

The ancient Egyptians buried their dead with food to sustain them during the afterlife, and high-ranking officials received more lavish provisions.

In 1977, the Sadat regime removed subsidies on basic foods; bread riots ensued, Egyptians took to the streets in protest. The government immediately reinstated subsidies.

———

Food unites families: the highlight of Ramadan, the holy month of fasting, is breaking the fast with relatives and friends at sundown. At the end of these evenings, guests wish their hosts many more meals, "Sofra dayma." Hosts respond with hopes for many more years of life, "Damit hayatkom."

Food affirms, or disrupts, marital bliss: a couple's decision on whether to have their customary Friday lunch with the wife's or husband's family is a familiar conflict. Nihal always diagnosed incompatible couples by saying that each came from a different dining table.

When my father died, friends and relatives, as dictated by tradition, cooked the lunch that took place after the burial. The day after his death, Bolbol sent over his preferred cut as a tribute: without writing.

Food, cooks, and eating were among the preferred subjects of Egyptian proverbs, which were the preferred vehicles for spreading wisdom across generations. On being once burned, twice shy: he who burns his tongue from soup will blow into yogurt to cool it. On hospitality as friendship: an onion offered with love is as satisfying as a leg of lamb. On karma: one who cooks poison tastes it. On striking first: eat him for lunch before he eats you for dinner. On the importance of a warm welcome: a heartfelt greeting is better than lunch. On one who forgets the kindness of others: he eats and denies.

Recipes, like popular sayings, were passed on without writing. As older generations passed away and younger relatives rejected culinary traditions, these recipes were forgotten. The few women who were granted the opportunity to transcribe what they knew remained fairly niche, like Abla Nazeera and her *Principles of Cooking*. Her influence on successive generations transformed the culinary industry, but she's rarely credited for having done so. Somehow, her words and her legacy remain confined to the realm of the kitchen, fodder for housewives undeterred by her demanding, labor-intensive recipes.

Fatma was illiterate and memorized recipes. She had no use for measuring cups, preferring to rely on her senses. Her power in our kitchen, and in our home, came from the elusive nature of her knowledge. My mother's friend spared no detail but withheld one ingredient to guarantee her dominion. Each of these elisions relates to power: granting it, securing it, protecting it. In a country with a tendency for censorship, there's a peculiar irony, and subversion, inherent to keeping secrets—if you don't transcribe a record, it can't be destroyed.

It was a cookbook that took me to the censor's bureau. On a molten Sunday morning in the summer of 2004, when I considered myself well-read but not well-versed in life, I received an angst-ridden call from our freight forwarders. In the two years since the inception of Diwan, we had been exposed to situations that we never anticipated would accompany our relatively docile career of bookselling. In the making of Diwan, Hind, Nihal, and I remade ourselves. Immigrants new to the land of business, we quickly realized that if Diwan was going to survive, we would have to adapt to our new world. We all understood that we depended upon a shared ecosystem of support and strength. This was especially true in the more alienating settings, like business, bureaucracy, and government: structures we would come to know well.

As Diwan's sales had grown and our readers' tastes had expanded, so had our import of books from abroad. According to the freight forwarder, one of our shipments from the United Kingdom had been delayed in customs because it contained titles deemed offensive to "public morals." The person responsible for the shipment—me—was asked to visit the Mogamma', the main government administration building, in Tahrir Square (where, seven years later, the Egyptian revolution would unfold).

The request prompted me to visit my lawyer, Dr. Mohamed, for advice.

"Ustazah, there is nothing to fear. They just want to get to know you. Diwan's reputation has grown in just two years. Your path was bound to cross with the censor's. Think of it as a dog sniffing someone visiting his master's house," he said, trying to pacify me.

"I'm uncomfortable with what I do not comprehend and cannot navigate." (My formality here is purposeful—it's general practice to maintain this kind of decorum when speaking to male "authority figures.")

"Then your stay on this earth will be a troubled one. Trust in the will of God." He asked Adham, a junior partner from his office, to accompany me on this "friendly" visit to the censor.

President Mubarak was proud that under his governance, Egypt was a country free from censorship. This meant that we were permitted to speak or act as we chose, provided it was within the law. As law-abiding citizens, we knew that it was illegal to say, write, or print anything that offended

public morals, threatened national unity or the social order, or tarnished Egypt's reputation in the foreign press. Violating these rules could result in imprisonment, payment
of fines, or the suspension of licenses. Mubarak ran our
lives, and our homeland, under the guidance of a tried-and-
tested Egyptian proverb: strike at the shackled and the free
shall be deterred.

In 2008, the opposition journalist Ibrahim Eissa was
sentenced to two months in prison on charges of offending
the president after writing about Mubarak's ailing health.
Civil lawsuits were filed against him, and the issue received
substantial media coverage. Mubarak eventually pardoned
him. As a respected and influential member of the fourth
estate, Eissa was never going to jail. It was a performance
meant to remind everyday citizens of the government's power
to punish. I used to think that the arbitrary ways laws were
enforced, and the opacity of the laws themselves, were accidental. But after almost two decades of conducting business
in Egypt, I know it's by design. The pervasive uncertainty
and endless delays are tools for control. You watch from a
distance, knowing that one day, your turn will come. Until
then, you surrender to panoptic self-censorship, measuring
your words.

My driver, Samir, was a seasoned navigator of Cairo's
chaos—on the day I was scheduled to visit the censor, he
zipped through the packed streets of Mohandiseen. Calls
to prayer, emanating from towering minarets, echoed
around the city. They didn't deter Samir from pelting the
occasional choice word or phrase through the rolled-down
window. These ranged from "You donkey!" to "Ya Khawal!"
to my personal favorite, "You are lower than a razor blade

strewn on the ground." Samir's deepest contempt was for the microbus drivers who were known to drive under the influence of any drug that would numb them out of existence. I didn't notice a difference between the microbus operators' hash-fueled disregard for human life and other drivers', mine included.

This disregard extended to pedestrians. I yelped as a man sprang out of nowhere and hurtled through the traffic to cross the street. Samir barely missed him. Cairo doesn't have crosswalks, so pedestrians need Olympian skill to survive, let alone get anywhere: jumping onto moving buses, making space for more passengers, and then disembarking in the midst of other vehicles in full motion. Traffic lights flash one thing; traffic police officers dotting the intersections signal another. Chaos. We used the streets for protest, whether collective or individual: our disregard for traffic rules was a kind of civil disobedience, as was our creative relationship to bureaucracy.

Samir was one year older than me. I joked to friends that aside from my father, he was the only man who'd ever been useful to me. For me and many others in my socioeconomic cluster, having a driver in Cairo was essential. In Egypt, a deeply classist society, the differences between how people live are irreconcilable. Samir paid my bills: phone, electricity, water, and land tax. He renewed licenses and memberships. He dealt with government offices. All these responsibilities involved fan-shaped lines and delicate ecosystems of personal relationships. Since I spent most of my time working, Samir had become my replacement: he completed my to-do list; he got my groceries; he haggled with Bolbol the butcher; he dropped off my ironing at Akram's shack on the other side of Zamalek and arranged for it to be delivered when he knew I would finally be home.

If I didn't answer my phone because I was in a meeting, my mother would call Samir, and he'd give her my schedule for the day. On the mornings I started work before eight thirty, he drove my daughters to preschool, bought them chips against my wishes, and ensured they didn't leave their lunch boxes in the car.

Samir felt entitled to offer his unsolicited opinion on most subjects. On my troubles with Number One: "The shade of a man is better than that of a tree." With the caveat, "But a woman like you provides enough shade for herself and others around her." On employees who stole from the company: "A dog's tail will never straighten." On giving people second chances: "All the fingers of one hand are not the same." We spent hours together in Cairo's traffic, driving between meetings around the city. Samir knew more about me than Number One, the father of my children, did. He overheard all my phone conversations, rife with confessions, arguments, and insults. Occasionally, while I was on the phone, he would tap the glove compartment in front of me to interject his comments in a whisper. He was cheeky, slightly daft, and no amount of my criticism dampened his spirits. Despite his sloppy appearance (waddling walk, overgrown mustache, greasy black hair, and chipped front tooth), Samir was surprisingly calculating. With time, he became aware of the power he wielded from listening in on other people's conversations, and he learned when to dispense, and when to withhold, information. I trusted him. In a society that thrived on gossip and the bartering of information, he guarded my secrets as though they were his children.

Samir pulled up and parked in a third line of cars under the office of Adham, the junior lawyer. As we waited, without turning on the hazards or turning off the engine, Samir

got out, lit a cigarette, and offered one to the traffic policeman who'd walked up to threaten him with a fine. He gestured at the running engine, pointed to a random window
in the building, lit the second cigarette, and lodged it between the traffic policeman's fingers. They chatted.

I remained in my preferred place: the front passenger seat.
Women and employers normally sit behind the driver, establishing distance between boss and worker. I could have set up
camp in the back, but Adham would perceive sitting with a
woman as immodest. Offering him the front passenger seat
would be equally disruptive of unwritten norms. As a guest,
he must be given the most comfortable seat: the back one.

We crossed Kasr al-Nil Bridge, entering downtown.
Samir and Adham discussed the state of things: power cuts
in the poorer areas of the city, the rising price of a kilo of to-
matoes, and the latest rumors surrounding Mubarak's son,
Gamal, the heir apparent of the Arab Republic of Egypt.
We turned right at Tahrir Square onto Abdelkader Hamza
Street, where the Mogamma', the complex that housed
Egypt's bureaucratic headquarters, towered over us with
elephantine grayness. I'd visited the building as a teenager,
when I'd lost my national identification card. It had taken
me a full month to acquire my birth certificate, file police
reports, and prove to the state that I existed, during which I
learned the essential skill of bribery. The trick was to make
the proposal ambiguous, in case it raised suspicion. Giving
too little was an insult; giving too much paved the way for
exploitation. When I finally completed my application, I
slid it under the teller's partition with a twenty-pound note
inside. It was approved. In the years following, I came to understand bribery as its own act of civil disobedience: a tryst
between citizens and bureaucrats, spurning the official government systems we all work within.

If buildings hold memories, I hoped Mogamma' al-Tahrir had lost its. Occupying the site left by the demolition of the British barracks in 1945, the concrete leviathan was meant to serve as a centralized administrative complex where citizens could efficiently complete all bureaucratic matters. Its 1,309 rooms served more than twenty thousand people every day. It was a building only architects could admire, an icon of monotony and the death of individuality. (The Mogamma' was actually the color of sand, but I remember it in monochrome gray.) Kafka writes: "Every revolution evaporates and leaves behind only the slime of a new bureaucracy."

We were directed to the ninth floor, the headquarters of the Censorship Bureau. I placed my handbag on the belt of the security scanner and looked up at the arches above me. We turned right toward the sweeping staircase, its weary and dusty steps leading upward. Following gendered conventions, Adham walked up in front of me. It would have been inappropriate to go in front of him and give him a view of my behind going up the stairs. That was the privilege of strangers.

I proceeded through the floors: passports, licenses, birth and death certificates, and pensions. The musty stench of wet carpets. The sour scent of sweat. On the ninth floor, we were told that the office had relocated to the thirteenth. When we reached the office, I watched Adham as he approached the *farash*, asked for directions to the toilet, and slipped him a five-pound note. I pretended not to notice. A few minutes passed and the farash ushered us into the bureaucrat's office, to the metal chairs facing the desk. Mubarak gazed out at us from a framed photograph, customary in all government offices. Adham spoke in dulcet tones, reminding the official that we were here at his kind invitation to address a delayed shipment for Diwan Bookstore.

If bribery was a skill, the handling of government bureaucrats was an art form. As a woman, I had to show deference to his institution, and to his masculinity—but I couldn't show fear, which might imply wrongdoing. Adham spoke on my behalf to avoid antagonizing the bureaucrat. He flattered and cajoled him, carefully establishing an alliance.

The bureaucrat's fingers sifted between his files, pulling out an orange-colored invoice. I recognized the penguin at the top of the page. The censors knew Penguin as the publisher of *The Satanic Verses*, but we'd never dared to order that book. I mentally flipped through a Rolodex of Penguin books, searching for the offending title: *Lolita*? *Lady Chatterley's Lover*? It couldn't be *Nineteen Eighty-Four*, as that had already passed through several shipments. Finally, the bureaucrat presented Adham with the invoice showing one highlighted title and an illegible phrase scribbled next to it in Arabic. As Adham handed it to me, our heads leaned in toward each other. While the bureaucrat returned his attention to the open files, we turned to whisper to one another.

"Ustaz Adham, the title isn't literal."

"What do I tell him?"

"What I told you."

"Wait, what did you tell me?"

The bureaucrat muttered to himself some Islamic phrase about patience, cutting our dialogue short.

"This is not what we expect of a company with Diwan's reputation, nor from a young woman," said the censor, acknowledging my presence for the first time.

"Of course not. As you well know, ya basha, Diwan is an institution that aims to educate and enlighten the minds of all Egyptians. We are here to serve you in your admirable goals." Adham looked at me, inviting me to speak, but I couldn't. He exhaled and charged ahead.

"Basha, in Egypt, we pride ourselves on our women. They make good wives and mothers. You know how important it is for some of them to keep up to date with the latest trends going on abroad . . ." Adham trailed off. I fixed my gaze on the carpet, trying to distinguish the designs from the dirt. I rubbed my thumb against the gold band on my ring finger.

"At the Censorship Bureau, we have our finger on the pulse of the entire country. We know the trends before they happen," responded the bureaucrat.

"You know, in the West they have loose morals."

"Yes, it is deplorable. Look at their women. How does their God accept them?"

"Alhamdulillah 'ala kol shay'," proferred Adham.

"Alhamdulillah 'ala kol shay'," confirmed the bureaucrat.

"In America, everything is about sex and nudity. They don't have the wisdom of Islam, or the Censorship Bureau, to protect them," Adham continued while the bureaucrat nodded in dismay. "This is why they have to resort to such cheapness to sell books. But who are we to judge? As the Prophet, peace be upon him, said, 'You have your religion; I have mine.' You know, ya basha, there is nobody naked inside the book. Can you believe the maskhara? *The Naked Chef* by this Jamie Oliver—it's just a cookbook! But what can we do? We live in trying times, and now the internet is in our homes spreading more evil."

As we gathered ourselves to leave, Adham promised to send coloring books for the bureaucrat's children, in thanks for the honor of his acquaintance. I knew that when the next shipping holdup inevitably arrived, the office would just call us. With the censor's concerns allayed, I continued to stock an array of Jamie Oliver titles as soon as they were released: his return, his dinners, his kitchen, his Italy, his different ingredients. Our alliance had helped me survive the early years of marriage, of domesticity. His recipes allowed me into the kitchen I'd been afraid to enter.

A few years later, as a more seasoned bookseller, I walked into the offices of a different government complex the day before the national holiday celebrating the Prophet Muhammad's birthday. Samir followed me, carrying a stack of boxes of "sweets of the birth." These were typically comprised of a selection of sugar-coated sesame, pistachio, and almond bars, and Turkish delight. There was also a doll known as the bride of the birth and a sultan on a horse, both made of sugar. Samir stationed himself at the corner of the booths, leaving me to walk to the center of the room.

"Sabah al-fol! I need to finish this power of attorney before midday and I know how busy you all are. As a token of our respect, Diwan Bookstores would like to offer each of you a box of sweets to enjoy with your family," I hollered across the open space, gesturing toward Samir, who comically paraded the stack of boxes with an inviting smile. The cycle of paperwork was initiated and completed within twenty minutes.

"This will help you keep your figure," Samir told the full-bodied woman who sat behind the cashier guarding the open drawer of crumpled Egyptian pound notes in lieu of a safe. "For once make your wife a happy woman, instead of walking in empty-handed," he jested as he laid the box of sweets on a three-legged stool next to one official's desk with a smile.

Though Diwan was not a huge financial success, it was a moral victory, an experiment in marketing, and a mastery of the will. Hind, Nihal, and I ran a high-quality, labor-intensive operation and cut no corners. We had one location, with a handful of staff to cover the fourteen hours we were open every day. A lot of the behind-the-scenes work we did ourselves. Often, in order to break even, we sacrificed our own paychecks in the service of lowering operating costs. Perhaps, at some level, we did this because we still doubted our own value in the business we had created.

Against all odds, we had proven to our doubters and detractors that a modern bookstore could survive in Egypt. And as with all pioneering endeavors, ours had paved the way for others to follow. Imitators and knockoffs had begun to sprout up across the city. As we slowly lost business to these new stores, which undercut our prices by a pound or two, we were faced with a choice. We could let these copies, which were sincere in their imitation of Diwan, but not in their commitment to reading, crowd out our flagship. Or we could raise funds for an aggressive expansion, and attempt to pluralize what was singular. We wanted to expand our reach, and yet we didn't know whether we could possibly replicate the magic of our first shop while maintaining its authenticity. The success of the first store didn't necessarily mean that another one would survive. Even though none of us said it, I knew we were also worried about taking on more responsibilities. Our lives were already imbalanced enough.

We had dreamed of a bookstore. That dream had been

realized. Why weren't we content? For the first time, we found ourselves at odds with what we thought was best for Diwan. Consensus, our familiar terrain, evaded us. Steadfast Nihal wanted things to stay as they were. Ambitious Hind believed expansion was the only viable path: go big or go home. And I believed whichever one of my partners I'd spoken to most recently. Like our old cook, Fatma, who'd become domineering and intense after her promotion, I was changing alongside Diwan. At first, these changes were small. I urged Nihal to fire underperformers without giving them a second chance. I began to obsess over sales. Suddenly, most of my relationships revolved around shared to-do lists. I knew there was a middle ground, between benevolent bourgeois housewives and sales-driven tyrants. I hoped to find it.

One thing was clear: if Diwan was going to survive, we'd need to compromise on our ideals. I'd already started, as in the bureaucrat's office, where I'd made myself smaller and let Adham speak on my behalf, man to man. I knew that was the only way to rescue *The Naked Chef*, and myself. This was a minor sacrifice, but what might happen as the stakes got higher? What would I give up to get shit done? What would I surrender of Diwan?

4

BUSINESS AND MANAGEMENT

In the end, Nihal was the one who discovered our next home. She pulled Hind and me aside one day to make a confession: she'd gone to a real estate agent's showing of a beautiful 1950s modernist three-story villa. "With a garden. Off Heliopolis's main road. It felt like Diwan. You have to see it." She was still hesitant about trying to replicate the originality and intimacy of the flagship. We'd all agreed that if we ever opened a new location, it would need to be far from Zamalek. So we'd narrowed in on Masr el Gedida (New Egypt), an affluent neighborhood also known as Heliopolis, Greek for "sun city." Built on the outskirts of Cairo in 1905 as an escape for the rich, Heliopolis was founded by the Belgian baron Édouard Louis Joseph Empain, who settled in Cairo after meeting and falling in love with a local socialite, Yvette Boghdadli. Rumor has it that he built Heliopolis for her.

"You believe in it. It came to us. We should go for it." With Hind's words, we were off on a journey from booksellers to businesswomen. That week, we visited the villa. Tucked away from the main road, yet still visible and inviting, it had an air of humble grandness. Above a modest garden, a set of stairs led up to the main entrance. I felt certain after entering the building through the arched doorway. It just felt right. We could imagine our future there. The rooms seemed to invite these musings. Looking up at the intricate, vaulted ceilings, we pictured the mahogany shelves and stainless steel skirting beneath them. The high, lofty space was practically begging for ornate lighting; later, after we closed the deal, Minou designed a custom chandelier printed with Diwan's calligraphy, which we suspended in the center of the winding staircase. In short, we fell in love. And like people in love, we succumbed to fantasies. Of wanting more, of conquering space, of actualizing dreams, and of testing ourselves and our luck. Months of planning, paperwork, licensing, decoration, meetings with Minou, and the hiring and training of new staff followed. We created a new bag featuring Heliopolis's architectural marvels: the Hindu-style palace of Baron Empain, and the Belgian architect Ernest Jaspar's Heliopolis Company buildings with their fusion of Islamic and Art Deco architecture.

On Saturday, December 8, 2007, five years and nine months from the opening of Diwan Zamalek, we officially opened our second branch. It was a feat such as no one in Egypt had ever seen, an act of utter lunacy: a three-story villa filled with books. We designed Heliopolis with Zamalek in mind, striving for continuity in our sections and café, while also modifying our store for the new neighborhood. As we shuffled old and new hires between the stores, sibling rivalries ensued. Some staff believed the original would always be better; some wanted to prove themselves through the new store. Hind, Nihal, and I tried to channel this into healthy competition, while panicking at what was happening inside our Diwan family.

The three of us juggled new responsibilities, spending entire days in the Heliopolis café, just as we had done in the early days of Zamalek. We weathered terrible traffic in our hour-long trips along the 6th October Bridge between the two stores. On these daily commutes, my car became a makeshift office, too. As our work increased and our time grew scarce, Hind, Nihal, and I realized that we couldn't make every decision together. We needed to delineate our responsibilities more clearly.

Nihal took over managing the two cafés, staff, maintenance, interiors, and the stationery and impulse sections. Hind oversaw store operations, the warehouse, and all things Arabic (books, music, film). And I supervised our English and French books, marketing, and finance. We each gravitated to what we loved, while also agreeing to take on some of what we hated (see: "finance").

As Diwan grew, the three of us struggled to keep up. The workload, already daunting, doubled. We made small mistakes. We put our faith in staff. Most were dedicated, but some were dishonest. A few stole from us. All the while, we doubted our own abilities. In our later years, we'd make bigger mistakes. We'd increase our losses. We'd write off these losses.

As our shelves multiplied, stocking them required more vigilance than ever. As soon as I restored a section to neat equilibrium, a customer would inevitably disrupt the system: transplanting irrelevant books and discarding unwanted titles in haphazard stacks. Still, I took pleasure in correcting the disarray, with one exception: Business and Management. Despite, or maybe because of, owning a business, I had no interest in reading books about the subject. Diwan's customers clearly did, though. Business books flew off the shelves. Faced with growing demand, I divided and expanded the area into subsections: Finance, Management,

Marketing, Personal Growth, and Success Stories. As I became inundated with books by authors I had never heard of, I invented a game: I judged them as I imagined my father would have. I knew that he would have admired Warren Buffett (American investor and currently the fourth-wealthiest man in the world) and Robert T. Kiyosaki (the author of the Rich Dad, Poor Dad series) for prioritizing financial well-being over social status. I could imagine his distrust of business consultants and professors, like Jim Collins, Stephen Covey, and Philip Kotler—he respected knowledge gained through practice rather than theory. He would've scoffed at quick-fix books like *The One Minute Manager*, since he knew that complex problems demanded comprehensive solutions. I smiled when I imagined my father's distaste for one of our top sellers, *How to Win Friends and Influence People*. He didn't give a fuck who he offended, or how.

Over time, I noticed a strange discrepancy. People bought business hardcovers. In our other sections, hardcover sales were confined to the likes of J. K. Rowling and Dan Brown. Unlike Americans, Egyptians seldom bought hardcovers—ours was, and is, a price-sensitive market. Most of the population could barely afford to buy paperbacks. Most Egyptians struggled to afford food, clothing, housing, education, and health care. If there was anything left over, it wouldn't be spent on books. And the economy was still recovering from 2003, when the central bank "floated" the Egyptian pound, releasing it from the established exchange rate with the dollar and allowing it to fall in value. A popular saying summed up the situation: the eye desires what the hand cannot grasp. So even fewer people were buying pricey hardcovers, except for business books. I wondered why. Were these tomes essential office décor? Did businessmen display them like framed college degrees, imbuing their enterprises with an aura of success and scholarship? Was there an underlying assumption that businessmen could afford to spend money on books?

I walked to Hind's side of the Heliopolis store for answers. Her Arabic business section was stacked with translations of my English-language bestsellers. Arab authors writing about business were curiously absent.

"Can I help you with something?" Amir, Hind's Arabic-book buyer, asked with a smile. Once a *darbuka* drummer in a traveling band, Amir was handsome, with a towering build, ripe-date complexion, slicked-back hair, and wire-rimmed glasses. Still, his most striking attribute was his quick wit. He seemed to charm everyone he encountered.

"Yes. Where are the Arab authors who write about business?"

"There aren't any. Come on, Ustazah, lead the way!" he quipped. "Jokes aside, there's Ibrahim Elfiky, but he writes more about personal development, less about business."

"Don't customers ask for local authors?"

"No. They want the foreigners." Amir's gaze narrowed as he mused, "I don't think they would trust the advice of a local. They want the Americans who made it big." The customers' skepticism was well-founded. Nasser's reforms had sequestered businesses, promising collective ownership with the people. Once-thriving enterprises became inefficient bureaucracies saddled with people who felt little agency, or ownership, over them. After his election in 1970, Sadat, attempting to salvage the failing economy, instituted Infitah, literally "openness," an open-door policy that appealed to private (mostly foreign) investors. Mubarak, the next president, began a privatization program further aimed at divesting state ownership from the many businesses that had diminished in value due to poor management and corruption.

Amir continued. "Hard work won't get you anywhere, but bribery will. We've learned to be suspicious of businessmen, because we see them as fat cats who amassed their wealth through dishonesty. Success is not something we celebrate. We envy it, but we know it was gained unethically." He paused, as if answering a question. "Pray that Diwan coasts along. Don't wish for it to become too successful." His words echoed my father's repeated warning: "In this life, keep your head down and hope nobody notices you."

I thought of Amir and my father as I attempted to stock new business titles. At the same time, the project grew more personal. Once a compulsive reader of fiction, within the first five years of Diwan, I had begun to capitulate to the pressures and demands of my new persona as a businessperson, a label that became more adhesive as the bookstore grew—with our new office, new staff, new sections, and now, new location. I tried, and failed, to see myself as a businessperson. As usual, I read in search of answers. Surprising everyone, but most of all myself, I became one of Diwan's dedicated consumers of business and management books, hoping that their pages would offer guidance. (My experience with nonfiction had previously been limited to gender studies in college.) The books failed to capture my imagination, but I kept reading, fueled by insecurity, in the hope of self-improvement. I was never good with numbers. I preferred words. I knew nothing of business plans, bottom lines, top lines, and management lines. I knew that lines were things I crossed.

As I read, I encountered my nonexistence. The books were oblivious to my cultural context; people like me had gotten lost in translation. None of these authors provided strategies for navigating Egyptian bureaucracy. Standardized guidance, like budget advice, failed to accommodate the idiosyncratic nightmare of creating systems from scratch (like ISBNs and sales figures), surrounded by chaos. What piece of advice could help me deal with the fact that every shipment that entered Cairo Airport took anywhere from one week to three months to clear, depending on the tangle of regulations, missing paperwork, capacity, and staff? How could I ensure stability when everything that should have been a fixed cost was a floating variable? How could I handle a workforce that would rather be employed by the government, a boss that would pay less but also demand less? Or customers who expected Diwan to be a library, and tried to return books after reading them? Practical tools were useless in an impractical landscape that seemed to follow only one rule: *insha'allah, bokra, maalesh*. The words play on bureaucratic responses to requests: if God wills it, tomorrow, never mind. And then there was the added dimension of gender. These male authors, businessmen, and entrepreneurs came into this world never questioning that it belonged to them, whereas even in my own shop, I sometimes felt out of place.

I wondered if the books worked for my customers. What lessons did they learn? Many Egyptian companies were one-man shows, driven by a strong male leader. Ours was a culture accustomed to pharaoh figures. Delegation was seen as a sign of weakness, putting you at risk of getting ripped off. Maybe elsewhere, people understand that collaboration enhances efficiency and gives workers autonomy. In theory, I agree, but I struggle to delegate. I can't blame this on my being a control freak. I became controlling for a reason: I couldn't trust others to do my job to my standards. Perhaps the level of excellence that I sought was impossible to achieve. Only Hind and Nihal understood why I still insisted on stacking books myself when I had so many other responsibilities: most of my staff would avoid alphabetizing titles. For them, it was enough to dust the shelves and walk away. Since I was unable to rely on others, all tasks took on equal importance: both the mammoth and the minuscule kept me up at night.

I faced my own success and recognition with ambivalence. I shared Amir's distrust of the former, and I recalled my father's warning against the latter. But I was actively grappling with both. The Zamalek shop had a growing international reputation, with more tourists shopping daily alongside our regulars. Heliopolis was a larger store, a physical manifestation of our success. Suddenly *I*, as Mrs. Diwan, was seen as successful, too. And the visibility that came with being Mrs. Diwan was a little oppressive. Maybe it was a language problem: new words, titles, and identities failed to convey reality. On the one hand, I felt validated—noticed, witnessed. Can success exist if no one else sees it? And on the other hand, I felt terror at having my greatest ambition wrested out of my head and into the world. The incredible vulnerability of making a private thought public plagued me, and was compounded by the new shop. I couldn't be in two places at once. I had to let go. I asked my friend Yasmin for advice. She told me to stop thinking. "Thought belittles. Thought is a distraction. Understand that a thought is just a thought. You've always made a lot of noise. Accept quietness. Let go of old narratives that no longer serve you. I promise that new ones will appear." As I immediately wrote her words down on my to-do list, she snapped, "Oh, for fuck's sake! Maybe if you stop doing, you might start being."

I remember an ill-fated meeting one summer morning in 2008 with a man who wanted to franchise Diwan. It was exceptionally hot. Samir had parked far away. As I entered the grounds of the Heliopolis shop, I felt that my appearance reflected the sun's fury: pink cheeks, damp hair. I'm an aggressively punctual person, and I loathe people who are habitually late. I checked my watch to ensure that I was a few minutes early for the meeting. I stood at the steps leading up to the villa. I decided to take a tour of the back garden to check the cleanliness of the outdoor café, knowing that only desperate smokers would be occupying its tables on a day like this. Satisfied, I made my way up the stairs of the villa, passed through the arched doorway, and stood in the hallway, savoring the air-conditioning. Surveying the display opposite the cashier terminal, I saw books in disarray. I registered the disorder with disapproval, then began climbing the winding staircase to the second floor, circling Minou's suspended chandelier. On the surrounding walls hung portraits of thinkers and doers across disciplines, times, and places, also designed by Minou: Sheikh Muhammad ʿAbduh (Egypt's liberal Islamic reformer), Simone de Beauvoir, Marie Curie, Mahatma Gandhi, Pablo Picasso, Malcolm X, Mayy Ziyadeh, and many more. As I entered the café, I saw Nihal at a center table, deeply absorbed in *The Power of Now*. My eyes were always drawn to hers, which were patient and green. She inserted her bookmark into the well-thumbed pages and laid the book to rest on the table.

"Why can't our staff understand that well-arranged displays are pleasing to the eye? They enable customers to see, and maybe, hopefully, fucking buy a book, so we can pay their fucking salaries!" I complained. "I thought the books at the entrance were bad, but the ones near the stairs are stacked like a fruit seller's pyramid of oranges. We just went over this last month."

"Talk to Marketing and stop micromanaging." Nihal's expression stayed placid. She poured water into the empty glass before me. "I love Eckhart Tolle. You should read him."

"My bedtime reading is *How to Write a Successful Business Plan* and *The Seven Habits of Highly Effective People*. I've just finished *Who Moved My Cheese? An A-Mazing Way to Deal with Change in Your Work and in Your Life*. And guess what? I still don't like change. And I like self-help books even less."

"Don't allow your passion for Diwan to kill your passion for reading," she said, tapping a small brown glass bottle into the palm of her hand. She unscrewed the lid and administered five drops into my water. "We are successful as we are. One can only plan so much."

"You know I don't believe in this homeopathy crap." I picked up my glass, watching the drops dissipate.

"No matter. It works regardless."

"I'm not sure these business books help. They don't speak to me or my circumstances."

"Then go back to reading fiction. Maybe for you there's more truth in it."

"Where's the franchise guy?"

"The traffic is terrible."

"Unless he's a tourist, he fucking knows that as well as we do."

"Hind isn't here yet. You can fuss about that," Nihal teased.

"Hind has trained me, and all of us, well over the years. We know what to expect from her," I said, resigned. In her lifelong rebellion against our father, who saw punctuality as a prerequisite to personhood, Hind has never been early, let alone on time, to a single event in her life. Growing up, I always returned home five minutes prior to any curfew our father issued; for Hind, a schedule was a random assortment of numbers designed to be disregarded. To this day, we travel separately to the same meetings. I insist on being five minutes early and she doesn't mind being five minutes late. We fight.

As the minutes passed, I caught one of the customer-service staff's eye and directed his gaze to the offending displays. Shahira, our longest-serving Zamalek manager and the one who'd investigated my ballerina, kept reminding me to take it easy on our new hires. Heeding her advice, I tried to breathe out, then I channeled all of my frustration toward this staff member, glaring blatantly at the book displays and back at him. Finally, I marched over to make my distaste known. When I returned, Nihal was chatting to a young man dressed in a comically ill-fitting business suit with broad shoulder pads and cropped pants. He had an uncannily white face, brown eyes, and a substantial beard without the accompanying mustache. There was something insincere about him. Even the looseness of his clothes felt affected.

"The traffic must be terrible this morning," I opened, with a salvo rather than salve. He smiled but didn't apologize. We offered him tea, coffee, or Turkish coffee. He declined, and then began to speak.

"Diwan has become a household name in no time. I never imagined that Egyptians read so much, or were willing to spend their money on books."

"The saying goes, 'Egyptians write books, Lebanese publish them, and Iraqis read them,'" I countered. "We've created an experience, and that's why we are a success."

"Sorry I'm late," said Hind, casually breezing into the last vacant chair. She stared intently at our guest, urging the meeting to continue uninterrupted.

"Yes, and you set high standards. One of my favorite business gurus says, 'Good is the enemy of great.'" He leaned back, as if pleased with his own cleverness.

"Mediocrity is our enemy," I said.

The man cut to the chase. He asked us to imagine a world overtaken by Diwans: mini Diwan caravans in rural areas; kiosks in malls; smaller outlets in universities and middle-income neighborhoods; and even stand-alone Diwan cafés. I reminded him how small we still were, with only two shops and a five-year age gap between them. Still, there was something so alluring about imagining a regional Diwan takeover.

"The scale you are suggesting is a little . . ." I trailed off, allowing my silence to speak the rest.

He was undeterred. "Now is Diwan's moment. Remember what Jack Welch said: 'Control your own destiny or someone else will.'" I hated the idea that anything coming out of this guy's mouth could be insightful.

As our sycophantic visitor detailed the art of franchising, the modest fee his company would take, and the service to God and country we would be doing, Nihal listened earnestly. She was probably practicing the mindful acceptance of her then guru, Eckhart Tolle. Unwilling to forgive the man's tardiness, I kept glancing at my watch. At the forty-minute mark, I closed my notebook. I dropped it into the open mouth of my bag, curled up beside me like a lapdog. He paused. "I see that I have taken up too much of your time. Here's my card. Think about my proposal, and I'll be in touch." On cue, Hind, Nihal, and I stood up; I extended my hand to shake. He looked at my hand, looked back up at me blankly. I kept my hand outstretched. He offered me his elbow. My head tilted quizzically.

"I don't shake hands with women." One, two, three, four, five seconds passed. Then I forced a broad smile.

"Hug, then?" I suggested. He turned, flustered, and exited in a huff. None of us considered walking him out. Our laughter resounded through Diwan's café. I wondered if it followed him down the stairs. I didn't care.

"And to think you were offended that he didn't apologize for being late!" Nihal slapped one palm against the other in disbelief, her eyes glinting with mirth.

"Personally, I'm disappointed you didn't just hug him," said Hind.

"Or elbow him in the face! Maybe homeopathy does work?" I suggested gleefully.

As we collected our belongings, Nihal spoke what I was thinking: "How does a man attempt to franchise a business founded and managed by women, and yet think women are unworthy of a simple handshake?"

"Because he can," said Hind, zipping up her bag with a finality that put an end to both laughter and further discussion.

In hindsight, I realize that we should have read the signs: the large beard without a mustache, the trouser legs cropped to avoid touching the dirt of the ground. Both were in accordance with what Salafists believed to be the Prophet's sunna. Salafism, a revivalist movement within Sunni Islam, developed in Egypt at the end of the nineteenth century in reaction to Western imperialism. It advocated for a return to the early years of Islam, during which "purer" forms of worship were commonplace. But this was three years before the revolution, and we hadn't met our fellow Egyptians yet, so signs of religious allegiance went unnoticed.

The Mubarak regime was hegemonic in its support of mainstream Islam. Members of other religious factions practiced blending in, revealing membership through subtle signals only their brethren could read. They existed quietly, spreading their regimented religious practices, waiting for their day to come. And it did: with the fall of the Mubarak regime, groups whose relation to Islam was tenuous at best revealed themselves and the extent of their power. In the thirty years of Mubarak's reign, I didn't know anyone who had voted for him, or voted in general. Yet at the end of every election, he was returned to power with a 97 percent victory. In 2011, when he was ousted from power and unrigged elections and referendums began to be held, we all realized how little about our countrymen we really knew. But it would be some time before we'd be forced to face the full meaning of that rejected handshake.

Hind, Nihal, and I were three very different managers. I am not good at people. If Diwan's success had been dependent on my ability to win friends and influence others, we would have failed miserably. To be clear, I was a bitch to work with. I know, I know, it's a bad word. But I reclaim it with pride. I am a difficult person. I am not easy or simple. I missed the memo that suggested I should be. I was—and it's gotten worse with age—an impatient, exacting, and dictatorial leader. I was tactical, exerting pressure on those who worked with me and driving them to do better. I apologized for none of it, since whatever I asked of others, I demanded of myself first. Hind and Nihal understood that and let me be. Nothing provoked my fury like a half-assed job. Those who worked as hard as I did won my unwavering respect and loyalty. With those who didn't, I became notorious for my vitriol. I never grasped the extent of it until years later, when I discovered that I had earned the code name of "Terminator." Hind and Nihal dispatched me as their envoy to meetings with those they didn't care to see again; I was utterly unable to negotiate or mediate.

Inside Diwan, employees joked that the outcome of any situation was determined by which of us dealt with it. Hind, a woman of few words, was hard but fair. Crossing her was like being caught between a sword and a knife. A son of Ziad (one of the five founding partners) interned one summer at Diwan, stacking books and alphabetizing customer orders. He summarized our dynamic to his father: "Nadia makes a lot of noise, but Hind is the one who will quietly slit your throat." Nihal's subdued presence guaranteed she got her way, somehow ensuring that everyone left satisfied. And she celebrated others, like Shahira, who shared her compassion.

As our stock increased, we enlisted teams of data-entry clerks to work consecutive shifts in our "warehouse," the back room of our office in the Baehler mansions. The cramped room was filled with people at computer terminals, ripping through the contents of cardboard boxes, logging them into the system, then dividing the merchandise between Heliopolis and Zamalek. Mistakes ensued. During one of my mornings spent stacking and restocking books on the Heliopolis shop floor, I was infuriated to find that the books had been mislabeled and improperly fitted with security tags. I called Shahira, who, alongside her duties as Zamalek's manager, also trained new hires. I expressed my dissatisfaction and announced that I would be docking three days' pay from the data clerks. I immediately hung up, leaving little room for discussion. That afternoon, I passed by Zamalek to check on the shelves. Satisfied, I sat at one of the tables in the café, monitoring the flow of customers while working on my computer. Shahira approached me.

"I don't think you should financially penalize staff for small mistakes. It's a poor management strategy. It creates a culture of fear, instead of loyalty and creativity."

"Coddling may work for you. I hit where it hurts." I didn't look up at her. She sat down across from me.

"Tomorrow, none of the data-entry staff will be working their shifts."

"Why, did my discipline scare them away?" I asked, not meeting her eyes.

"No. I planned a retreat." I was incredulous. I knew that she read self-help books and that she believed in trouble-shooting through team-building activities and role play, but surely this was beyond the pale. I also knew she was in cahoots with Nihal.

"As you wish, but the docked pay stands. Now, kindly fuck off and go do something useful."

The following day, I stood in the street outside our office smoking a cigarette. Amir sauntered over to join me in the smokers' enclave. He placed a cigarette between his lips; I offered him my lighter.

"I'm guessing the day-trip wasn't your idea." He flashed a grin.

"One of the things I appreciate about you, Amir, is your love of gossip."

"And you, Ustazah, are a flexible dictator. Telling them to show up in jeans and trainers with a bottle of water, and then taking them out on a day-trip so they can play and bond, isn't your style. But you didn't get in Shahira's way. You let it happen."

"When I went into business, I never imagined I would have to mother so many babies."

"You aren't their mother. It's much worse: you are their nanny."

"And that's why I choose to be the pharaoh, cracking the whip," I joked as I flicked my cigarette against the pavement. "Shahira provides unconditional love and solves their problems."

"Her way works; your way works better. Men need to be treated like men, especially when their boss is a woman."

Men and their female bosses—sigh! As recently as the mid-1950s, when tensions ran high between Britain and Egypt during the Suez crisis, Nasser, in one of his infamous televised speeches, urged the British to mind their manners. A BBC program that referred to him as a dog had provoked his anger. His response? He reminded the British of the days when graffiti adorning the walls of Cairo and Port Said insulted them and struck at the core of their empire. The graffiti, which incited British outrage at the time, simply stated, "Your king is a woman." Sixty-five years later, this comment remains an effective taunt among Egyptian men. Sixty-five years later, the male imagination still cannot fathom a woman in charge.

Egyptian men in their twenties and thirties who had worked with me for several years struggled under my forceful reign. My unruly curly mane made obvious the fact that I didn't wear a veil, while also hinting at a wildness. My loud voice further defied expectations for female demureness. The staff respected me, but they had trouble reconciling my behavior with the model of respectable womanhood. Their respect was primarily economic. As one of Diwan's founders, I paid their salaries. But it was also personal. I never told my staff that they worked for me. Instead, I reminded them that they worked *with* me—even though, as I've mentioned, I was kind of a bitch. I knew that a great deal was lost in translation between my male staff and me. We came from, and inhabited, two different Egypts. They were rural boys who had migrated to the city looking for work; I was a city girl, born and bred in Cairo. They were predominantly Muslim; my family was one of mixed faiths. They graduated from government schools; I enjoyed the benefits of a private education, paid for in foreign currency, and had two master's degrees. My brazen confidence unsettled them.

They were unsure of how to respond to orders from women, because the only women they knew were their mothers, who doted on them, or their wives, who obeyed them. In Nihal, they found a gentle mother figure whom they were eager to please. She took an interest in their problems and tried to help their sisters, brothers, and cousins find employment at Diwan or in businesses run by friends. Diwan became a family affair. Most staff members had a blood relative somewhere in the company. Samir's cousin worked as a security guard in Heliopolis; and Abbas, Hind's driver, had four cousins scattered among the two stores, the company office, and the warehouse. Well before becoming Hind's driver, Abbas had worked as Nihal's cook. She still raves about his pasta béchamel. Nihal's cousin Nehaya, an eccentric, iron-willed, German-speaking tour guide, became our multimedia and stationery buyer. Nehaya and Shahira were old friends. As with most families, secrets never stayed that way, and gossip worked as currency. When staff were sick and needed more than government medical care, Nihal leaned on friends and acquaintances to make referrals for private doctors. When circumstances were dire, she would suggest that we managing partners split the cost. When Diwan was still small enough, we would close the shop one evening per year (we were open all other evenings) and take the entire staff out for *iftar*, the meal traditionally shared with family and friends during Ramadan in which the fast was broken. We never charged it as a company expense, because we saw it as our duty, and our staff as an extension of our family.

Though they loved Nihal, the men were confused by Hind. Her silence proved unsettling, especially when combined with her perceptive eagle eyes and the tales that began to emerge of how swiftly she dealt with those who defied her. Her severity was accentuated by Amir, her assistant, who exuded humor and delight. When work took her outside of the Baehler office, he accompanied her. Amir was there to lubricate interactions and execute decisions made on store visits, where she inspected the Arabic section, tested customer-service staff on the manuals she had prepared about new Arabic releases, and met with publishers to discuss the exposure their books got and negotiate discounts and credit terms. Despite her reserve, Hind's humility and politeness were endearing: she stood up to shake hands with customers and staff. She always introduced herself as Hind, eschewing any title, which, in a classist society, completely defied convention.

I'm not entirely sure how the male staff saw me—it's hardest to see oneself. I expect they noticed my aggression and humor. I didn't care. I did hope that my hard work, the only honest currency I knew, would make up for all my shortcomings. When new shipments of books arrived for stacking, I carried the heavy boxes alongside other staff, against the grain of workplace hierarchy and gender roles. When maintenance staff didn't clean the toilets properly, I grabbed the brush and did the job myself as a lesson in standards. I knew a male boss wouldn't have carried out the demonstration, especially with a task as demeaning and domestic as toilet cleaning. Even when I was pregnant, I kept up with manual labor despite the extra weight. I was a sight to behold: a thirty-two-year-old, outspoken, formidable, box-heaving bookseller. And they gaped! I was too young to resemble their mothers, and too old, by Egyptian standards, to be pregnant.

The tension between my male staff and me finally came to a head one chilly Sunday morning in January of 2006. I was walking down 26th of July Street to the office, wearing dark-blue maternity jeans that chafed against my protruding belly button. They were the only pair that still fit me. A black sleeveless bodysuit kept my spilling flesh together. On top of that, I draped an oversized black knitted cardigan with a huge collar, hoping to offset my own bulk.

I clutched the strap of my computer bag for balance and strength. With each step I took, I said to myself: I will go to work, no matter how uncomfortable, how vulnerable, I might feel. I'd already been pregnant once before, with Zein, but I hadn't felt as overwhelmed, depleted, or imbalanced then. And I worried people noticed the difference.

Right outside the shop, a young man approached me, smiling, a *Thriller*-era Michael Jackson T-shirt hanging from his scrawny torso. Judging from his age and stonewashed jeans, he might have been a teenage school dropout, maybe apprenticing with a mechanic or a plumber. Delicate beads of sweat gathered on his forehead. He came closer, close enough for me to smell his odor mixed with lemony cologne. He said something, and I pulled my earphones out to hear. He probably had a question about Diwan. Without slowing his walk, he casually repeated, "You got fucked well, you naughty girl." Blood rushed to my ears. My vision faded to pulsing red blotches. All I could feel was heat. I mustered as much force as my crippling rage would permit and yelled, "Yes, I got fucked. I spread my legs just like your mother did, and she gave birth to a little bitch of a cocksucking slimy wad of discharge masquerading as a man." Profanity gushed out of me like air from an untied balloon. The young man took off in a sprint. I tried to run after him, but my swollen body slowed me down; I became angrier at my anger for stealing my breath, angrier at my body for immobilizing me.

Two of the shop's morning maintenance crew witnessed the scene from the foyer, which they were cleaning. I pointed at the man disappearing down the street, but he was already gone. They rushed to me. With one hand, I clasped the chrome handle of the open door, trying to prop up my crumpled body; with the other, I tried to hoist my computer bag onto my shaking shoulder. I looked away from the street and into the bookstore, following the shock wave of my outburst. The morning-shift staff looked at me as if I were a stranger who resembled someone they had once known. Clad in Diwan uniforms, one stood with a pile of books in hand on a wobbly ladder, while another held the ladder in place for him. Everyone was suspended in time, speechless. The cashier with gift vouchers in his hand turned away to stare into his till drawer. The security guard, who normally stood by the metal detectors to make sure thieves stole from us in only modest amounts, made the first move.

He pushed a chair toward me, its legs screeching across the floor, and gestured for me to sit. Legs apart, arms slumped behind me, I tilted my head back, taking in air with ragged gasps. I steadied myself by looking over the spines that lined the surrounding bookshelves: each one seemed to symbolize a choice I'd made. Soon, I began to panic again, as I realized the repercussions my words had already had: I watched my enigmatic, bookish persona recede, replaced by a foul-mouthed wreck. I had poisoned my professional image of eloquence and literature with my gutter vocabulary, a language my staff had never imagined I spoke. (This might surprise you, since I swore all the fucking time to Hind and Nihal, but I mostly kept the habit from my staff for the sake of decorum.) I couldn't undo this. My only option was to pretend the confrontation had never happened. Addressing it directly would, I was sure, be construed as weakness, or worse, regret. I wanted to talk to Hind, but I knew she would tell me to pick my battles and conserve my energy. I decided to talk myself through it first: this story would make the rounds to the evening staff, and to the main office, each person embellishing it with fabricated details before passing it on. It would probably circulate to neighboring shops: the Bank of Alexandria on the corner, Thomas Pizza next door. Somewhere along the way, it would inevitably be replaced by fresh drama—embezzlement or some sort of side racket parallel to the business. Egyptians love excitement, and nothing is as exciting as the petty transgressions and private lives of others. So, I set it aside, a little pleased that Samir would be devastated to hear of this episode secondhand.

That afternoon, I met an old friend in Diwan's café.

"You said what?" she squealed with laughter, her hazel eyes tearing up. She tried to breathe deeply, looking at my bulging stomach pushing against the edge of the table. Another fit of giggles followed as she imagined the scene.

"Would you calm down? You're embarrassing me in my office," I said, conscious of the disapproving stares coming from surrounding tables.

"That ship sailed this morning!" she laughed. Eventually, her giddiness subsided, and she sighed. "Thank you."

"For what? The comic relief?"

"For calling him out. Do you know how many times I've been harassed, and then told by well-meaning friends and family that responding would be unladylike? Women need to talk back."

"Still, I need to stop this story from spreading. I don't want my mother to find out, or I'll never hear the end of it."

"Tante Faiza would be proud. She wouldn't say so, but she would be." She hesitated. "Once she gets over the shock."

I felt outed, my secret, dirty lexicon forced into the open. But my friend was right: the self-exposure brought an unexpected relief. That Sunday morning proved to be a turning point both in the way I regarded myself and in the way others regarded me. As the story of my vulgar retort made the rounds at Diwan and beyond, I was met with a new degree of respect. Still, the admiration was complicated. Only when I took on behaviors associated with masculinity, like swearing, did my male staff see me as one of them, and thus deserving of their respect. Had I somehow bought in to their patriarchal norms? I crossed one line, only to find myself hemmed in by another.

I did feel relieved to let go of the urge to apologize for swearing, or for being myself. Slowly, coarse language became a source of power. Each curse was a minor rebellion against my family, my class, and the pressures of gender. As decorum loosened its grip, I felt myself becoming myself, resisting the expectations of my staff, and even of my father, a frequent swearer, who'd warned against visibility. I thought of Amir's response to my employee discipline. I had learned a Machiavellian lesson about managing men in this society: inspiring fear was more important than inspiring admiration. With time, I learned to deploy this power strategically, in doses. Curse words were like an arsenal of nuclear weapons: when everyone knows you have them, you don't need to use them.

It was around this time that others—publications, customers, and acquaintances—bestowed a new label upon me, one familiar from the shelves of the business section: entrepreneur. Like all other labels, I bristled against this one. I wanted to know how other women navigated leadership and professional power, so once again, I read. Before the twentieth century, women initiated small business ventures to supplement their income or to replace the income a spouse would have contributed. Because their primary responsibilities were to their children and their homes, most of their economic pursuits had domestic associations: dressmaking, hair care and beauty products, housework, and midwifery. I learned about Sarah Breedlove, America's first female self-made millionaire. An African American entrepreneur, Sarah Breedlove created and marketed her own line of cosmetics and hair care products for Black women called Madam C. J. Walker (she'd changed her name when she married her third husband, Charles Joseph Walker). She died in 1919, leaving a legacy of activism and social work, as well as a fortune of six hundred thousand dollars, roughly the modern equivalent of nine million dollars.

She was an anomaly, a woman who miraculously transcended her womanhood. I imagined her on one end of the spectrum of female labor. On the other end stood the female workers of modern Egypt—mothers, daughters, abandoned wives, and widows who were constrained by their positions to varying degrees. One of these was Sabah, the woman who used to clean my apartment. I never knew her last name.

She'd worked for an American couple I knew, and when they left Cairo, they suggested I hire her. I accepted, but she hesitated. She didn't like working for Egyptians because in her experience they didn't treat maids well. When they told her Number One was American, she changed her mind.

Sabah was a spindly, flat-chested woman whose agility I envied. She had a sallow, sesame complexion. I only noticed her missing teeth when she smiled, which was not often. Sabah's cigarettes were her most treasured companions. She would sit on one of the kitchen stools, one heel nestled against one buttock, and take drags of her cigarette, speaking to it or to herself (it was always unclear which). Sabah led a dual life. Every day, she arrived at our apartment in a long-sleeved shirt and floor-length skirt with her head and neck covered by a colorful scarf bunched together under her chin. Once inside, she changed into a torn, oversized T-shirt and loose trousers with a low-hanging crotch and folded-up cuffs. She tied her hair up like Rosie the Riveter. When I offered to buy her a uniform, she refused. I explained that the staff of Diwan wore uniforms, too, and that I expected all workers to look presentable; work in any form should be done with pride. But she wouldn't budge. I assumed that Sabah told her neighbors she was a nurse, maybe because the occupation of house cleaner was low in the social hierarchy.

Sabah had the key to our apartment. She arrived around midday, because she enjoyed staying up late to watch television and because the red buses and minibuses that she had to take from the neighborhood of Haram, where she lived, were too crowded in the morning. She left the apartment whenever her work was finished. Our paths seldom crossed, but neither of us minded. Wiping the floor was her last chore. The first time I saw her drag the cloth with her hands in sweeping arcs, her body perfectly bent in two, I bought her a mop to make things easier. She thanked me, and proceeded to leave it in the broom cupboard untouched.

What I knew of Sabah's life I learned from Samir, who occasionally joined her for a smoke in between errands. I found out that her husband, unemployed, used to spend his days at the ahwa smoking sheesha. Eventually, he disappeared, lessening her burden but leaving her saddled with the certainty of being sole provider for her son and elderly mother. I knew that 30 percent of Egyptian households were headed by women (divorced, widowed, and single); they were the primary breadwinners. How distinct were their stories? Even worse, how similar? Weren't they all entrepreneurs in their own right? They had to creatively solve the problems of their daily lives, taking professional risks with uncertain consequences. Female providers were stretched beyond their capacity, but they coped, just like Sabah did—until, one day, an incident toppled the painfully delicate balance.

"We have a problem," hissed Samir from under his sloppily trimmed mustache, clearly relishing the drama of the news he had to relay.

"What now?" I asked, opening my diary, ready to add one more task to my list.

"Sabah's son is in jail. She needs cash, but she can't ask you for a loan."

"Why is he in jail?"

"I don't know," said Samir, feigning ignorance. I raised my eyebrows in dismay, and he revised his statement. "Well, of course I do, but Sabah would kill me if I told you, and I swore on the lives of my children that I wouldn't."

"Why won't she ask me for a loan?"

"She's already drowning in debt."

"She should stop spending on cigarettes, for a start."

"That's what people like you always say. You don't realize

that cigarettes are our only pleasure in life . . . well, and the other thing."

"What is she planning to do?"

"She is going to take a second job," said Samir incredulously.

"She can barely manage this one. There aren't enough hours in the day."

"I always say you are a woman who provides shade for others from the beating sun. Give her some of your shade."

Later that day, I had an idea, so I left the office early. I asked Samir to stop the car outside of a home goods store, where I picked up two nonstick cupcake trays. I returned home to find Sabah slumped at the kitchen table, the heaviness she always carried somehow even more pronounced. The only proof she was still conscious was the smoke trailing from her cigarette. When she registered my presence, she rose, beginning to tidy up aimlessly. I asked her to sit back down, and she obliged.

"There's a new coffee shop a few doors down from Zamalek. I know the owners, so I offered to supply them with carrot cake. I'll teach you how to bake it and price it out. You can do it here alongside your cleaning, and you can coordinate with Samir to deliver the cupcakes during his errands. To begin, I'll supply you with all the ingredients. Whatever money you make is yours. If things go well, you can start sourcing your own materials."

I knew I'd made an offer that she could finally accept. She hugged me across the kitchen table, and I felt the coldness of her bones. I realized that she was crying. I tore out a sheet from my notebook and passed it to her along with my pen so she could transcribe the recipe. She shook her head.

"You write it. Make it big and clear," she said.

Within two months, Sabah was purchasing her own

ingredients; she managed to scale her daily production up to 192 carrot cupcakes. The apartment smelled of cinnamon and vanilla icing.

I thought of other women whom life had condemned into nonexistence, beautifully bundled into Judith Shakespeare, the playwright's fictitious sister whom Virginia Woolf described in *A Room of One's Own*. She stayed at home while her brother went to school, her ambition hampered by gender. The necessity of her eventual marriage made any career impossible. Could Sabah have been Madam C. J. Walker instead of one of the millions of Shakespeare's sisters with their thwarted destinies? Why are female entrepreneurs understood as only a contemporary phenomenon? Stilted historical narratives and cultural mores deny our foremothers' labor—domestic, professional, and otherwise—in favor of progress, suppressing untold narratives and preventing us from knowing what we are capable of.

And why is it that when I look to my entrepreneurial ancestors, I am met only by Walker? Again, there's the problem with a single narrative, even when that narrative is a trailblazing one. Where are the Egyptian women in charge? Sabah's life was constrained not only by the broken systems surrounding her but also by the absence of precedents in our collective imagination. And even when they existed, some chose to be portrayed as men. Take Hatshepsut, the fifth pharaoh of ancient Egypt's Eighteenth Dynasty, who was regarded as one of the most successful rulers, focusing more on trade than conquest—statues of her with a male body and a false beard abound. The belief that women in charge in big business, small businesses, women who manage, don't exist, when, in fact, they've been present throughout history, is crippling. Hind was named after one such woman, the daughter of Utbah ibn Rabiah, a very powerful woman in early-seventh-century Arabia, who owned more than one hundred camels. Still, she is remembered primarily as the archenemy of the Prophet Muhammad, and as a powerful man's daughter.

Another powerful woman from our canon, Khadija, is primarily defined and remembered in relation to men and their institutions. First known as Khadija bint Khuwaylid, then as the wife of the Prophet Muhammad, she was born in the latter half of the sixth century into a family of merchants of the Qureish tribe that ruled Mecca. She enjoyed tremendous respect and a reputation for fairness. Khadija inherited a fortune from her parents and continued trading and increasing her wealth well after their deaths and the deaths of her first two husbands. Stories suggested that her camel caravan surpassed the length of all others that traded with Syria and Yemen, the commerce centers of the time. She hired Muhammad to oversee one of her caravans to Syria, and he impressed her with his honesty and diligence on the job. She was forty and he was twenty-five. She sent a mutual friend to ask for his hand in marriage. It was her immense wealth that furnished him with a room of his own during his early prophethood. That's where he meditated, received the word of God, and questioned the validity of his revelations. It was her faith in him that made her the first convert to Islam and enabled him to venture out as the messenger of God. She managed him then, too, calming the stress and pressure of his newfound role. Theirs was a monogamous union that lasted twenty-five years and produced four daughters. It was only after her death in AD 619 that polygamy, a common practice at the time, seems to have crossed his mind. He subsequently married ten women, not including concubines.

Despite her widespread influence, Khadija is mostly remembered as a dutiful wife. I didn't know her full story until I was an adult. Her historical mistreatment resonated with my contemporary encounters, like with the franchiser who couldn't shake women's hands. If the Prophet Muhammad was accepting of his wife's powerful status, how could this franchiser, so eager to replicate the practices of the Prophet Muhammad's time, find us so unworthy? So many men spend their lives studying holy books with the hopes of becoming holier themselves. But they apply these religious texts to justify bad behavior, while secular men pose as moral authorities to pursue the same cruel goals. Our beliefs insulate us from other people, blinding us to our own hypocrisy.

Of course, these rules apply to women, too. While the scarcity mindset encourages competition, it also stifles solidarity. Life had confirmed Virginia Woolf's claim: "Women are hard on women. Women dislike women." Even though this happened more than ten years ago, I can't rinse it out of my memory. A well-put-together middle-aged lady came up to me on Heliopolis's shop floor as I was stacking books and arranging displays.

"I want to speak to the owner."

"I am one of them," I said, as I set down the batch of books in my hand on a nearby table.

"You must be the secretary," she scoffed. "Now run along and find me a decision maker." I stomped up the stairs to the café, ordered myself a coffee, and returned the calls of the day that I had missed. By the time I ventured back down into the book section, she was gone. I didn't know whether her assumption was based on the menial task she'd seen me doing. I didn't know whether her terseness was evidence of patriarchy's indoctrination or her own desire not to see fellow women succeed. Whatever it was, it stung because it came from a woman.

Despite the overwhelming work required by our new branch, we'd already begun discussing opening another one. We were ambitious, we were hungry, and maybe I was cocky. Anything seemed possible. There was also an altruistic force behind the new plans: we wanted to make more of an impact on a greater swath of people. In the midst of all this growth, I'd given birth to Zein and Layla less than two years apart. This brought more labels: pioneer, successful, mother, working mother. I struggled to recognize myself in these identifiers. I hoped that I would be able to in retrospect. Notions of power and success struck me as narrow, restricted to "real" professions rather than unpaid feminine labor. Domestic work, the work of giving care, went unrecognized, so whenever I was applauded with an award or a profile pertaining to my work in Diwan, the validation felt hollow.

In 2014, I was contacted by a journalist at *Forbes Middle East*, who was part of a team compiling a list of the two hundred most powerful women in the Middle East. I was ranked at number sixty. I asked how they measured power; they told me it was a complicated matrix of factors. For men, they ranked wealth: still complicated, but a more blatantly numerical rubric. I wondered why.

They invited all of us powerful honorees to an awards ceremony, at the One&Only resort on Palm Jumeirah, an artificial archipelago in Dubai. The hotel was swathed in so much splendor that it felt like a caricature of itself. I walked down marble corridors until I reached the tongue of red carpet, which was bordered by photographs of the honorees. More marble, gold, nacre, and alabaster surrounded the ballroom. Flowing orchids crowned elaborate table settings. This was a wedding with many brides, their maids of honor, and too few grooms.

I assessed my fellow powerful women with excitement. Most of them were accompanied by their best friends, daughters, or mothers, and I felt a pang: I should have brought Hind or Nihal, perhaps even my mother, who always managed to instill my moments of triumph with her own bittersweetness. Like the time in 2011, when *Time* magazine interviewed Hind and me, and featured a photo of us two "unlikely entrepreneurs." My mother's pride at her daughters' *Time* debut was hampered by the untidiness of my eyebrows.

"Darling, couldn't you get them done?"

"Actually, Mum, had my appearance been a factor in my success, I promise you, I would've addressed it long ago."

Faiza's criticism aside, I did feel unkempt and underdressed as I scanned the other women's clothing, from the Princess Jasmine–like ball gowns, to more traditional Emirati dresses and abayas, to business suits. I wore a khaki silk wraparound dress and sensible ballet flats. I was introduced to a TV presenter who towered above me, swaying like a pendulum in her heels. She maneuvered me to one of the backdrops, positioned me at an angle with my left foot forward, and began interviewing me on camera. I chastised myself for not bothering with foundation or powder, which I only ever applied at weddings: my face would look shiny in the footage, in contrast to the interviewer's matte complexion.

A booming voice announced the arrival of Sheikh So-and-So and the start of the ceremony. Powerful women were ushered to seats at the front, their plus-ones to tables farther back. The lights dimmed; dramatic music and a laser show followed. Eventually, I heard my name called. I rose, climbed onto the stage, shook the sheikh's hand, received my gold-inscribed glass plaque, smiled for the cameras, and descended. Once all the awards had been distributed, I placed the cold plaque between my palms and treaded, hunched down in the dark, to the back of the ballroom to make a discreet exit.

In the months and years that followed, I returned to the feeling of awkwardness that clouded that night. All these women being celebrated for their power by other women, with hardly any men in sight, other than the sheikh giving out the awards. I guess we didn't need to say what we already knew: that most celebrations of women aren't something that men feel comfortable participating in. In my early twenties, I attended many stilted International Women's Day celebrations. The few token men present always said something hyperbolic and ingratiating, which only accentuated their visible discomfort.

Weeks after the ceremony, I received a poster-sized photo of myself captioned *The Most Powerful Women in the Middle East* above the *Forbes* logo. My tightly crossed arms suggested both strength and confinement. My daughters were so proud of me that they decided to hang it in the kitchen, next to the refrigerator and above the garbage bin.

5

PREGNANCY AND PARENTING

The shelves of Diwan were the first to know of my pregnancy, after Hind and my mother. From them, I surreptitiously plucked *What to Expect When You're Expecting*, and then I went back into hiding. I approached change with caution, like my mother. I remember summarizing the book for her—how it said I would feel, the bodily changes I could anticipate, the dos and don'ts that accompanied this temporary upheaval—as she looked on, dismayed. At some level, I knew that I was trying to control the uncontrollable. I hoped that if I could itemize my pregnancy on a to-do list, I'd feel autonomous again.

"I remember being pregnant with Hind, sitting in the doctor's waiting room for hours, smoking to pass the time."

"You smoked?" I asked her with horror.

"Of course I did. And I didn't give up my Scotch. The doctor told me that quitting smoking or drinking would add to my stress. I had my trinity to help me through: Virginia Slims, Johnnie Walker, and Dr. Spock's *Baby and Child Care*."

"At least you read," I said, convincing myself that one good habit out of three made for an acceptable record. Our conversation illustrates a generational divide. At the start, Diwan didn't have an elaborate Pregnancy and Parenting section, which I'd learned was a necessity from research-ing online and visiting bookstores abroad. But our culture complicated this necessity. In Egypt, where extended fam-ilies live close together, pregnant women are cared for and guided by their mothers, families, and female neighbors. Parenting has historically been a communal affair. We learn from others, not from books.

Indeed, Hind's Arabic inventory corroborated this fact, featuring only a single shelf stocked primarily with encyclo-paedias of children's names.

"I read Dr. Spock to guide me through your early years, not to tell me that my stomach would stick out!" my mother responded with exasperation. "My mother died when I was sixteen. She took her advice with her." My mother's own ad-vice had shaped my buying habits yet again—I ordered Dr. Spock's *Baby and Child Care* for Diwan that day. Published in 1946, it had become one of the bestselling volumes in history, not too far behind the Bible. Dr. Spock assured women that they knew more than they knew: he encouraged them to fol-low their instincts, to be affectionate, and to listen to their baby's needs. His gentle, approachable tone paid off. By the time I read it, sixty years after its publication, the book had been translated into forty-two languages and had sold more than fifty million copies. I heard echoes of my mother's ad-vice in Dr. Spock's no-nonsense guidance.

"But did you exercise at all? Yoga, maybe?" I remember asking her. What had begun as a search for advice had be-come this extended bonding exercise between mother and daughter. What I hadn't expected was that I would end up espousing my mother's worldview, since I had spent most of my life rebelling against her.

"Exercise? I can hardly listen to you." She paused, and tried to explain. "Pregnant French women don't stop eating

Brie, and Japanese women don't quit sushi. The only thing you need to exercise is your common sense." At the time, I thought her attitude was a relic of her era. Now, I wonder if she was right.

I always left our exchanges with the same question: How "common" is common sense, really, across a divide of three or four decades? I gave birth to my first daughter, Zein, in 2004, my mother to me in 1974, and her mother to her in 1933. Aside from our shared genetic lineage, what did our experiences of giving birth have in common? My mother's mother, Fotna Wahba, gave birth to six children over the course of fifteen years, beginning in 1926. She had all of them in her Zamalek apartment overlooking the Nile, with the help of Ayousha, her midwife. Two of the six, twins, didn't make it: the boy died after three months; the girl, more resilient, lived an additional three months. My father's mother, Susannah, a green-eyed redhead from a tiny village in Mansoura, the first outpost of Napoleon's cultural invasion of Egypt in 1798, began her childbearing career around the age of sixteen, giving birth to my father in 1921. This work spanned fifteen years and yielded eight or nine children, all delivered at home by a midwife. The head count varied depending on who you spoke to. My father and his siblings were lucky to survive the malaria and cholera epidemics that swept through Egypt in their youth. Like so many women who weren't from the upper or middle class, Susannah lived and died without a surname any of us could remember.

By the 1960s, the standard shifted from home to hospital births. The process was streamlined for maximum efficiency. There were an increasing number of cesarean section births, including my sister's and mine—my mother, like so many others of her era, had little say in the matter. And it's only gotten more pronounced: in Egypt today, a whopping 52 percent of all hospital births are cesarean sections (as opposed to around 30 percent in the United States according to the CDC).

"I was so thirsty after I regained consciousness. I begged the nurse for water. She just looked at me and said, 'Do I look like a fucking water wheel?' I was alone, your father was traveling, I was scared, and I was at the mercy of that pest."

"So what happened?"

"The next nurse who came to check on me was kinder and I was able to ask her if you had any birth defects. I was forty-one years old. Few women gave birth at that age. All my friends had their children twenty years before. And there were no ultrasounds. Things could've gone badly."

"Not because you drank and smoked, but because you were over forty?"

"Exactly."

"You didn't even know if I was going to be a girl or a boy?"

"Folk wisdom held that mothers pregnant with girls got more beautiful, so I knew I was having girls."

Children rebel against their parents. My mother's class and generation had eschewed written guidance on pregnancy, whereas my generation was eager to know. That might explain the success of *What to Expect When You're Expecting*, first published in 1984, which paved the way for other maternity books. Throughout Diwan's early years, I witnessed an incredible surge of guides, manuals, and planners for how to wean, feed, potty train, put to bed, dress, raise, and discipline children. Some staked out specific markets by age group, number of children, and gender. All capitalized on this relatively new trend in global publishing. I cautiously stocked these books, developing my section, while trying to balance the perspectives they offered with the perspectives I'd grown up with. Could the modern obsession with having the perfect pregnancy really catch on in Egypt? It felt like a capitalist perversion of this basic experience of human life. I watched as the banality of parenthood transformed into a spectacle that justified the purchase of specific clothes, gadgets, and now, books.

When my mother had raised Hind and me, almost fifty years earlier, there were no disposable diapers, special colic-preventing feeding bottles, toys disguised as educational tools, or maternity clothes designed to flatter and conceal. The industry didn't exist yet. My mother, a seamstress by training and a die-hard devotee of sixties fashion, made her own dresses—maternity and mini. She also spent countless hours making reusable cloth diapers, which she then boiled to sanitize between uses. Even as the landscape began to shift around her, she remained steadfast in her beliefs. After Hind gave birth to Ramzi, her first son, my mother told the attending obstetrician that beer was the best stimulus for milk production—tried and tested by the ancient Egyptians. Later, while visibly pregnant with my second child, Layla, I sat down to dinner with friends at a New York bistro. I ordered a beer. The waiter declined to serve me. When I told my mother about it, she was appalled. Mothers of her generation saw no reason to change themselves just because they were embarking on a new phase of life.

When I was pregnant, people were always entering my space, touching my bump, offering unsolicited advice. "Breastfeed for the first two years!" "Don't breastfeed!" "Formula is liquid garbage!" "Stay active!" "Don't overexert yourself!"

I became fed up with all these contradictory remarks, the gadgets and guidebooks, which promised to empower me but really just made me feel claustrophobic. Maybe my mother knew more than I gave her credit for. I wasn't completely sold on her old-school ways, but I also knew that contemporary consumerism and perfectionism were no better.

"What about Dad?" I asked her once, in earnest.

"Ramzi?" my mother replied, now herself surprised. "Pregnancy isn't a man's concern." But of course this has changed. As I researched books to include in our Pregnancy and Parenting section, I kept seeing titles geared toward men. Titles like *From Dude to Dad: The Only Guide a Dude Needs to Become a Dad* emphasized the transformation inherent in "becoming" a father (the implied transition from "cool" to "less cool"—from "dude" to "dad"—wasn't lost on me). Other titles promised survival and salvation, like *The Expectant Dad's Survival Guide: Everything You Need to Know* and *Diaper Dude: The Ultimate Dad's Guide to Surviving the First Two Years*. The motif of the diaper (absent from titles geared at women), and the dude who wields it, attempted to infuse new paternity with humor. Another popular book, *Commando Dad: How to Be an Elite Dad or Carer*, imagined fatherhood as a battlefield, an appropriately testosterone-filled terrain. Of course, there were other books that attempted to induct men into this new phase of life less comically. But regardless of the tone, my mother and her generation found the mere existence of these books, and their underlying assumptions, bizarre. In the end, I didn't purchase books about fatherhood for Diwan. Stocking books about pregnancy was already enough of a gamble. I'd save my time and resources for titles that would sell.

———

Like so many of us, I often act without understanding why. Knowledge comes after the fact. While paying for my copy of *What to Expect When You're Expecting*, I muttered a forcibly casual remark to the cashier about how it was for a friend. Even as I said it, I didn't realize how much I wanted to distance myself from someone "expecting." I needed to figure out how I was going to acknowledge, or deny, my condition. Would I *lean in* to a new persona as pregnant boss? Or would I ignore my changed state? I quickly decided that I would work even harder throughout my pregnancy to set a good example. Perhaps I was privately afraid of what was happening to me, and I wanted to minimize it in the eyes of others. Of course, my body had its own plan.

When I hired new staff, I always asked them the same character question: What are your aspirations for your children? Answers ranged from "I want to raise a good Muslim," to blank stares, to "I want them to emigrate to a country where they have better chances."

There was another question I always asked: "If you were to join Diwan's family, would you be able to work the evening shift, or just the morning one?" We were open daily from 9:00 a.m. to 11:00 p.m., closed only on the morning of the first day of Eid al-Adha, so shifts were an issue. I also asked because I had become so used to Egyptians' demanding lives. Most of my male staff worked two jobs to raise their income, or took computer science courses on the side. Scheduling became nightmarish when we needed to move staff between the two stores to cover holidays or sick days.

"I can work as long as it is daylight," the female candidates would often respond. I knew the subtext: Respectable girls don't come home after dark. If they do, their neighbors judge them, and that judgment earns them a reputation that diminishes their odds for a good marriage. Also, being out of the home in the evening meant taking public transportation, where women were subjected to a near-constant barrage of harassment from drivers and fellow passengers. I was familiar with the compromises women made under patriarchy: they competed for their family's resources, subordinate to their brothers; they helped with the housework and took care of elders; they were limited in where they could go and who they could see. On top of all that, as my male coworkers liked to remind me, it was more financially advantageous to hire men. This is partly because Egyptian labor laws grant women ninety days of paid maternity leave for their first two children. Men have more working hours, especially since the basic concept of paternity leave is nonexistent in Egypt. It struck me as ironic that the very laws that attempted to guarantee women their rights—like paid maternity leave—also exposed them to discrimination. Even though hiring women could be a pain in the ass, I chose to do it anyway because I am a woman and I pay it forward.

I was uncomfortable with the assumptions that our culture made about women: that motherhood would, and should, eclipse any other responsibility. In my case, it hadn't. When I was first pregnant, with Zein, I worked up until the day before I was scheduled to go to the hospital for my cesarean. I returned to Diwan three weeks later, eager to ignore the catastrophic instability of motherhood, eager for the order of the shelves, and eager for the familiarity and security of work.

Some of these feelings only came to light through a conversation with a total stranger. In 2008, I was interviewed by a women's magazine on having it all, "it" meaning a successful career and a family. My actual situation was far less glamorous. I was divorced from Number One, juggling two- and four-year-old daughters—and a six-year-old Diwan. We'd just opened our third location, in Maadi, a suburban district ten miles upriver from Zamalek. The neighborhood was replete with lush green spaces. Its affluent inhabitants included a sizable expat population. As a litmus test for the location, we'd opened a small stall in the recently constructed Carrefour City Centre Mall. When that was a nearly instant success, we started looking for a brick-and-mortar space in Maadi, eventually settling on Road 9, the local equivalent to 26th of July Street. The area was known for its pedestrian traffic, so we took the first store we saw, despite its placement at the dodgier end. We gambled on our brand name, hoping it would pull people off the beaten path. But a few months after opening, we were second-guessing ourselves. Foot traffic was erratic and didn't reliably lead to sales—the expats seemed to prefer borrowing or exchanging books to buying new ones. And that was even before the full impact of the global recession on multinational corporations, many of whom housed their employees in Maadi. We were struggling to allocate staff and move merchandise among our three stores.

I'd agreed to meet the journalist at Maadi, in the new café. She had dyed blond hair and thick makeup. She was swaddled in a tight floral top with a black skirt. She arrived early and got on my good side. As soon as we ordered our cappuccinos, she began with the usual set of sterile questions: Where had the idea for Diwan come from? What were our biggest challenges? What was it like working with my sister and my friend? How did we resolve our differences? And then, she asked the inevitable: "As a woman, how do you reconcile the demands of home and work?"

"I don't." I swallowed. "I never will. I wouldn't trust

anyone who claims to have done so. No one asks men how they balance the demands of their families and their children with their professional lives. I'm a guilty working mother. I miss so many baths and diaper changes. My children's nanny is always there. On some days I get home so exhausted that I don't want to play with my daughters or read to them as they go to sleep. But I made my choices. I want my girls to grow up in a home where their mother works. I am a single parent, and I am proud and grateful." The journalist just stared at me, startled.

I'd been truthful with her, but not entirely honest. I didn't describe the depth of my angst. I failed to mention my inability to choose the right diaper cream. Or that I scrubbed the white line the cream left under my nails to remove any trace of contact. Burping Zein was a grand undertaking. I felt humiliated every time her burp evaded me. I held my breath while pressing the snaps of Layla's onesie together, praying as I worked my way to the bottom that I hadn't missed one, which would have forced me to start all over again. I dreaded the cries that I couldn't assuage or decipher. Even my triumphs, like sealing a soiled diaper symmetrically, felt pathetic to me.

My discomfort preceded motherhood, beginning when I was pregnant. I had become distanced from my body. I gained almost thirty pounds and my feet were heavy, like two soaked sponges. I grew even clumsier. I wish I could forget the day I had a meeting in Zamalek's café when I had a terrible bout of morning sickness. I excused myself from the meeting, ran to the bathroom, thanked God it was empty, and hurled myself at the toilet, just in time. Unfortunately, I hadn't had the time or foresight to take off my glasses and scarf. The glasses fell into the toilet in mid-vomit. The scarf was equally doused. I tried to salvage both, and then returned to my meeting, hoping that the smell was in my head. Times like these made me resent the images of maternal bliss I saw on the covers of pregnancy books. Where were the faces ridden with malaise and alienation? Where was the discomfort and dissatisfaction of breastfeeding? Why did nobody warn me about the additional guilt of harboring these feelings at all? On the nanny's day off, I used to take Zein to Nihal (whose kids were now teenagers), so that someone else could bathe and feed her. I didn't want to be left alone with her, to have to face my own incompetence. A decade later, I read *The Art of Hearing Heartbeats*, a novel set in Burma, which describes the protagonist's mother as having come into motherhood "empty-handed." Even though I had endless books and my own mother by my side, that descriptor seemed to sum up my feeling completely. "I'm sure your kids will be avid readers," said the journalist, trying to lighten the mood.

I wonder if there's a way I could have claimed pregnancy, and early motherhood, as my own, rather than constantly searching for advice, validation, and belonging. Maybe it is just an inherently unsettling experience. The only thing that made me feel like myself during those years was stacking books, arranging them on our shelves with care. I would forget my children, my failing marriage, the leak in the bathroom ceiling, the ironing I had to send to Akram (the laundry man who worked out of a shack on the corner of Bahgat Ali Street). I would surrender to a kind of transcendence that felt like drifting, surrounded by the abundant shelves, the ample conversation, the snippets of laughter. I belonged in Diwan, in a way that I didn't in my own home with my daughters. Even though I'd brought them into the world, I sometimes felt that their very existence diminished and threatened mine. Parenting continually brought my weaknesses and limitations into stark relief.

Part of my distaste was due to the expectation that childbearing would be the ultimate fulfillment of my womanhood, my crowning achievement. The assumption that selfless love and infinite sacrifice defined and delineated the meaning of my life, and the lives of other women. In that suspended state of purgatory, we were meant to leave ourselves behind. Bearing children signified success—never mind how they turned out. Despite everything I had strived for, how hard I had worked to create Diwan, I received the most lavish praise for becoming a mother. It reminded me of being congratulated for my marriage. I wondered if people married for love, or if marriage was the prerequisite to parenthood, the anticipated result for which we were preordained. My marriage had been intentionally childless for seven years. Were those years meaningless? No. They were happy and they were productive. I started Diwan during those years.

Back when Zein was two and Layla was eight months old, I'd turned to the shelves of Pregnancy and Parenting. My marriage to Number One had come to an end. I needed help seeing a way forward. Despite the massive catalog of pregnancy and parenting titles, hardly any addressed divorced or single parenting. I ventured to other sections for inspiration. Self-Help had a few books on happy marriages, but none on happy divorces. I retreated to novels. Maybe I should have stocked Pregnancy and Parenting with Ian McEwan's *Nutshell*, in which a fetal Hamlet overhears his mother's deeds and plots his revenge from the womb. Or with Margaret

Atwood's *The Handmaid's Tale*, where fertile women become breeders owned by wealthy families. We could travel further back in time to Greek and Roman mythologies, which acknowledged the pain and chaos of love, marriage, and parenthood more than any contemporary guidebook.

Of course, the family unit structures most novels. *Happy families are all alike; every unhappy family is unhappy in its own way.* Tolstoy's memorable opening line inspired the so-called Anna Karenina principle, put forth in Jared Diamond's 1997 nonfiction book, *Guns, Germs, and Steel.* The book argues that it's the absence of negative traits, not the presence of positive traits (à la Darwin), that guarantees a species's survival. The same could be said of marriages. We assume that happy marriages survive, and unhappy ones end in divorce. The persistence of a marriage constitutes a success, while divorce is a failure. Why? It seems to me that many divorces qualify as successes, while some intact marriages fail—to satisfy, to grow, to strengthen.

Why had my marriage failed in the first place? The tipping point occurred just forty-eight hours before I was due to deliver Layla. (This was a few weeks after I'd cussed out the street harasser and stunned my staff into silence.) It was Friday, and Fridays in Cairo always felt like hangovers. The pace was slow. The sounds were muted. I waddled down 26th of July Street holding Zein's hand, trying, and increasingly failing, to ignore the bolts of pain darting up my left leg with every step. Hind's silver station wagon pulled up alongside me. She waved Zein and me in. Even though my home was just a few streets away, it felt like miles, and I was glad for a ride. I buckled Zein into Ramzi's empty car seat in the back and took my place in front, next to Hind.

"I can't take much more. Get her out of me."

"She probably feels the same," said Hind.

"Don't you remember your last two days before delivering Ramzi?"

"Some things I've made an effort to forget." Hind, clearly eager to bring our testy exchange to an end, pulled up to my building garage, even though I usually entered the building from the front.

I remember noticing immediately that the apartment was eerily quiet. Zein let go of my hand and ran to her room, the patter of her footsteps fading. I made my way farther down the corridor to our bedroom. I didn't call out his name. I just pushed down the door handle. He was leaning against the green iron railing at the bedroom window, holding the phone to his ear, with his back to me. I didn't call out. I didn't move. His tone was mellifluous and sweet. I wasn't trying to listen, but I could hear everything. More than the actual words, his sweet tone, the looseness of his pose, hurt. I covered my ears, but it was too late. A hollowness set in. I looked to the floor, certain that my guts had fallen out and were piled in a heap. Finally, I asked him in a parched voice to stop talking. He turned around. He told her he had to go.

"I didn't see you walk into the building," he said defensively.

"I used a different door," I explained automatically. We left to attend our weekly family Friday lunch. I stole a moment with Hind to tell her what happened. Her pained look matched mine. I filled my already taut belly with food and drink. After lunch, I screamed at him, but I was really screaming at my own stupidity.

On schedule, two days later, I was wheeled into the operating room. He was there, looking at me beneath furrowed brow, with an inscrutable expression. I felt vacant. This was happening to someone else. I recognized neither him nor myself. At the time, I didn't want to be a divorcée, and I didn't want my daughters to grow up always feeling deprived of one parent.

As soon as my incision healed, I went back to work. Diwan had always cured my ailments, but this time was different. Whenever the subject of marriage or divorce occurred in a conversation or a book title, I felt hyper-visible. I didn't want to talk, or be talked about, until I could get my own story straight. I found myself wondering whether Sabah, our house cleaner turned carrot cake supplier, knew more English from her former American employers than she let on. She must have noticed that Number One and I no longer ate meals together. Or that our interactions had become polite but strained. I imagined her gossiping about it with Samir between his errands. In the car, I carried on my private conversations in French or English, languages Samir didn't speak—but I began to worry that he, too, had finally pieced together enough vocabulary to decipher sentences. I imagined it as if it were happening: Samir sipping his tea, telling a group of staff members on break about my marital woes with dramatic virtuosity. Every time I emerged from the office, I swore I saw a cluster of workers disperse. During the months that followed, whenever Samir drove me to marriage counseling, I'd have him drop me one street over. Then, for good measure, I would send him on an errand so he wouldn't be able to see the building I entered.

My paranoia increased. I had imagined conversations with the books of Diwan—increasingly with one specific author, Elizabeth Gilbert. When we'd first opened, Number One had discovered her first novel, *Stern Men*. He liked her voice. He urged me to order several copies. I remember standing on the shop floor recommending her to anyone who seemed curious, with no success. I brought in the cavalry: I stuck the *Diwan Recommends* sign on the untouched pile. Still nothing. Many months later, defeated, I tore out the title pages and sent them back to the publisher as part of our annual returns. I bore a grudge. I didn't like books that let me down. In 2006, the same year as Number One's revelations and our divorce, Elizabeth charged back into my life with the bestselling memoir *Eat, Pray, Love*, promising self-discovery after her own divorce. The book sold itself. Every time I passed the stack, or restocked it, whether in Zamalek, Heliopolis, or Maadi, the author spoke to me.

"Get lost. It's the only way you'll find yourself."

"Shut up, Liz! You don't know my life."

"It doesn't matter. Surrender."

"Fuck off. You know how your story ends."

Hind and Nihal never left my side. In the middle of meetings, I would glimpse them looking at me with concern. When they realized they'd been caught, they'd offer reassuring smiles. When that wasn't enough, they'd spell it out: *You will be fine, you will come out of this better and stronger, you aren't the first and you won't be the last. Shit happens.*

After six months of marriage counseling and infinite advice from close friends and casual acquaintances, I had to face my worst fear: disappointing my mother. Up to that point, when I'd brought up the affair and its aftermath, she'd only made cryptic comments. I assumed she disapproved. That was a small truth. The larger truth took longer to see, that mothers want better lives for their daughters than they had.

"Shall I make molokhiya or fatta for today's lunch?

What would the children enjoy more?" asked my mother on our daily morning call.

"I don't think the kids give a shit, Mum. They're eight months and two years old. Make fatta."

"Fine. I will tell Beshir to make molokhiya. Children should eat greens." Our conversations always followed this pattern: she asked for my opinion, I gave it, and she did what she wanted. "I had something else to ask you. Why are you still with him? Did your father and I raise you to eat shit and then stay for the second helping?" She didn't wait for my answer. "I have to go and talk to Beshir about the garlic, he didn't put in enough last time." The following day, I exercised the 'isma, a woman's right to divorce in Sunni Islam. While legally sanctioned, it was socially frowned upon: belly dancers insisted on the 'isma when they married. I got divorced not because he cheated but because he took me for a fool. And he was right, I was a fool. I'd never seen this coming. There was minimal recrimination. Neither of us wanted to be victims.

Maybe Liz was on to something. I had to surrender to what was. The next day at work, I casually announced that I had divorced, then noted how well the kids were doing, and how much they already enjoyed having each of us to themselves. At home, I opened myself to the emptiness of the flat, welcoming the quiet that had moved in. I reorganized my cabinets, filling the new space with my own things. I started seeing my old friend the Naked Chef again. On our regular dates, I cooked his recipes, artfully plated them, and then took the leftovers to the office the next day. I took comfort in one thought: when Zein and Layla were older, we would sit at the same table, share food and stories. There would be no leftovers.

Oddly enough, I found solace in my sorry state. I was a sympathetic figure, the wronged wife. I felt momentarily unburdened of the need to be strong. I'm sure people behind my back justified Number One's infidelity with my work/life imbalance. What else could a man do to a woman who didn't need him, aside from supplementing her with others who did? As time passed, I realized that I wasn't angry at the other women. They were free to do as they wished, and they weren't responsible for my disappointment. I was even more surprised by my lack of loathing for Number One, by how much I continued to cherish our relationship. Maybe his transgression was insignificant in the scheme of things. Perhaps my gratitude toward him outweighed the hurt. His actions, our demise, liberated me in a way I hadn't been able to liberate myself. In the ten years our marriage had thrived, I couldn't imagine myself fully outside its parameters. I'd left my younger self, the one he'd married, behind, but I hadn't fully come into my adult self. Now that I was released from my obligations, I felt freer to be my own kind of mother, my own kind of (ex-) wife, my own kind of person.

But I didn't really see myself as a "wronged wife" or an "ex-wife." "Ex" suggested a crossing out, an undoing. After the implosion of our marriage, we worked toward a new relationship. We didn't let our kids use the divorce to manipulate us. We stayed in close contact and compared notes. Of course, we still argued. About schools, sleepovers, and strategies for dealing with playground bullies (my favorite of whom was the son of a children's-TV producer, whose father threatened to send his driver to beat up Zein's nanny in the playground). But we learned to pick our battles until compromise became a habit. We each remarried. We each divorced, again. We didn't need to explain our failures to one another. Without realizing it, we had become friends and confidants, too aware of each other's flaws but still happy to ask the other to listen or to advise.

Fifteen years after we split up, despite the standard bickering, I had no doubt that we had become a successful failure: we were happily divorced. He read this book along with our daughters, Hind, and my mother as I wrote it.

We had made a deal. When the girls were old enough, we would tell them about the affairs. Then: "I know our family secret," said a precocious thirteen-year-old Layla.

"Just one? How disappointing!" I teased.

"Dad told us he cheated on you." She caught me off guard, as she'd clearly intended. Now she flashed me a coy smile, trying to gauge my response.

"Well done, Dad, for taking ownership." Of course, Layla was not satisfied. She wanted drama, embellishment, carnage. I wouldn't give in.

"I don't know what I would've done in your shoes," she said.

"You would walk. I walked for you, in spite of you. I walked away from your father and our marriage because I knew that one day you would ask, and I wanted to have an answer I would be proud of. You walk."

"Ending it must've been hard."

"Indecision and regret are harder."

"You must have some regrets. Aren't you scared of growing old alone?"

"Don't confuse being alone with being lonely. Some of my loneliest times were when I was in a relationship."

"Mum, is this one of those things you say that I'm gonna get when I'm older?"

"Let me make it simple. Never make a decision based on fear or guilt or guided by what you think is easier. Choose what rings true to you."

"Why can't you just admit it was tough, and it wasn't fair?"

"Very little in life is fair, but it is what you make of it. I am no trailblazing heroine, and I'm no better than the millions of women who stayed in shit marriages. I could afford to divorce. It was that simple. I had a roof over my head and yours and I was financially independent." I leaned forward to kiss her forehead. "And when I pray for you and Zein, I ask that you know what contentment and gratitude feel like, and that you grow to be confident and self-sufficient." Zein, like Hind, never broached the subject. Both of them prefer to reflect on things privately.

My no-frills approach to parenting stood in stark contradiction to the guidebooks. Throughout my daughters' childhood and teenage years, I was as blunt and candid as possible. When my daughters were younger and they would ask for some indulgence, ice cream or toys or a delayed bedtime, I would answer: "I want to say yes because I love you, but I'll say no because I love you more." My urge to please was secondary to doing what was best for them. I often told them, "As your mother, I can guarantee that I will love you unconditionally. But I can't promise that I'll always like you. You have to earn that." I still say this to them! And I still mean it. Authority and authorship are inextricably linked: we are responsible for who we become, and who we become is a deliberate act. My narrative for myself and my children still has no room for victimhood.

I can call our divorce a success, but I can't yet say the same of our parenting. I'm waiting to see how Zein and Layla turn out. The terrible truth is that how they turn out is completely beyond my control. Parenting, like authorship and entrepreneurship, holds no guarantees. Reid Hoffman, the cofounder of LinkedIn, famously uttered the phrase "An entrepreneur is someone who will jump off a cliff and assemble an airplane on the way down." Children, and other new ventures, are not issued with manuals. We embark on endeavors with some assessed risk, lots of hope, and the certainty that any plan will need modification, because so much can and does happen along the way. Diwan is a case in point: we created her exactly as we had imagined her, hoping she would fare well. To ensure her continued survival, we had to adapt her to our shifting world. Hind, Nihal, and I were often divided on decisions regarding Diwan's future. Now, all these years later, we agree it doesn't matter what or who was right or wrong—it's done. In the case of parenting, we don't learn the outcome of our efforts until well past the time to make changes, and we don't stop blaming ourselves or one another.

As I continued to read books and people over the years, Diwan, and Egypt, changed around me. As always, my shelves offered me an unexpected education on these changes. Reviewing publisher catalogs, I witnessed the increased diversity in pregnancy and parenting books, which shifted over time to accommodate political and social norms. Words like "family" and "childcare" began to proliferate, while "parent" transformed from noun to verb. A parent, once an authority figure who disciplined children, had become a mentor who holistically raised children as *individuals*. This was a departure from my mother's generation, who'd expected their children to be obedient. Girls looked after their parents, and boys carried the family name.

Brothers and sons were free from active obligation. Our generation expected our kids to be geniuses who would outpace us because of all we had given them. Our hope was rife with the pressure we unknowingly inflicted on ourselves and on our children.

This shift from parent as disciplinarian to parent as mentor didn't quite align with Hind's and my own upbringing. Our parents evaded categorization. My father was strict, but more indulgent than my mother. He'd always tell us: You are shit, unless you prove otherwise. And once you've proven it, wake up tomorrow and prove it again. The minute you think you've succeeded, congratulations, you have taken your first step on the path to failure. He was seventy years old when Hind and I were teenagers. As a survivor of lung cancer, he gave us daily lectures on the hazards of smoking. Drinking and gambling were fine. Conscious of his own mortality, he was determined we would flourish after his demise. In this, he unknowingly became a compartmental feminist: insistent on his daughters' independence in all aspects, while ensuring that during his lifetime his wife never had true autonomy. It was his training that made it all possible—Diwan and divorce.

My mother's parenting was stricter, as was her own upbringing. She attended the Mère de Dieu, a Catholic school run by nuns, then the Lycée Franço-Égyptien in Zamalek. At the lycée, she learned discipline, her love language; Arabic, her native language; and French, the language of her country's colonizers and of her own religious worship. My mother had little time for opinions or indulgences. Ours wasn't a family where adults asked children for their opinions; we were expected to obey. She never differentiated between Hind and me. As children, we received the same punishments and rewards. Her ruthless parity reminded me of an

Egyptian saying: equality in oppression is justice. Our leisure time was structured by her militant to-do list (I keep my own lists to this day). She aimed to educate us, and herself, taking us to every museum, art gallery, and theater in town. She collected the programs and saved them for when we were older; Hind and I do the same for our children when we drag them to cultural events against their will. As kids, we were so indignant about spending our summers keeping up with my mother's rigid regimen of cultural appreciation. Of course, as usual, she was right. She taught us to savor literature, music, art, and dance, and for that, I'm belatedly grateful. As time passed, I was able to see my parents' harshness for what it was: a surplus of love and dedication. They parented us strictly and gave us opportunities they'd never had, to raise not child geniuses, but survivors.

One of Diwan's bestsellers, Naguib Mahfouz's *Cairo Trilogy*, chronicles the lives of three generations of the family of Al-sayyid (Mister) Ahmad 'Abd al-Jawad in Cairo from 1918 to the 1952 revolution. The paterfamilias, a despotic patriarch who rules his family with an uncompromising severity by day, carries on affairs with dancers and singers by night. His intensity and hypocrisy are underlined by the infuriating docility of his wife, Amina, who patiently and dutifully waits for him to come home every night. She places a gas lamp at the top of the stairs to light his way up to his room, washes his feet, speaks only when spoken to, undresses him, puts away his clothes, and if nothing further is needed, retires to her room. She is up at dawn daily, praying, wakes up the maid and the children, ensures that all are fed and packed off to school.

Up until my twenties, I couldn't see my mother as a

person with her own ambitions and past experiences that predated me. In my twenties, I tried to get to know her. I began to confide in her. I expressed myself as I would to a friend, using the language that suited the situation. I swore. A lot. My mother never swore. In her recounting of the story of the nurse who denied her water, she could only refer to her as a pest—not the word I would've used. Reluctantly, she began to reciprocate, to tell me things about her life and her marriage that I'd never known. I started to wonder if I knew too much about my parents and their marriage. But then I realized that Number One and I had done exactly the same thing with our teenage girls.

As a parent myself, I began to confront this dissonance between mother and person. I saw my own friends set themselves aside for their children, neatly separating their identities. This got trickier as our kids got older, as less and less went over their heads. They understood what they saw and heard, like when Layla asked me about Number One's affairs. For better or worse, I never had the time to compartmentalize my various roles: I was the same Nadia with them as I was at work as I was at the bar with friends. I drank and swore in front of my kids as much as I did in their absence. In school, they had learned of the dangers of smoking and it terrified them. When I quit, I still had the odd cigarette, and I didn't hide in the bathroom like other mothers I knew. When they asked me about sex, drugs, and alcohol, I tried to tell the truth. I figured that I'd rather say too much than be forced to lie. I'm sure I've passed on my neuroses, like all parents. The more I looked for models, for advice, for guidance that would help me get it "right," the more I became convinced that trying to control pregnancy and parenting is a Sisyphean task. We try our best, hoping only to minimize damage.

While I could see my mother only as a mother, I failed to see myself as anything but myself. My mother always said that parenthood humbled her. It broke her and it built her. My father said it held him hostage. And finally, I knew what they both meant. Suddenly, there were two more people on this earth I'd happily give my life for. If I'd known the intensity of this commitment, I wonder if I'd have still chosen to take the risk of parenthood, to expose myself and others to the potential of so much pain.

Parenting, like marriage, is a power struggle. That ultimate managerial tug-of-war between mother and father. My parents succeeded in carving out domains, and they never trespassed onto each other's territory. After my father died, my mother conquered new terrain, filling the space that he left with herself. Her love for her grandchildren overtook her love for Hind and me, and she grandparented accordingly. She'd always snap at me when she sensed I was treating my daughters differently. I'd argue that they were different ages and had different privileges, and she'd inevitably tell me that her approach—to treat Hind and me as similarly as possible—was superior. I listen to my mother, but I don't always take her advice. In the same vein, Number One and I make the big decisions together, but we don't haggle over the minutiae. Our divorce, and the relationship it facilitated, freed us from the power struggle of daily shared parenting.

Control is the one addiction I have spent a lifetime trying to quit. I've been deluded into thinking that I can control anything, including my desire to control everything. The truth: most things that we care about are outside of our control. Deal with it. I have. I am. I remember lying on the cold steel table during Layla's birth. I knew relief was within reach. A hospital worker brought her to me for a kiss, then took her to a nearby table. I watched as they cut her cord and suctioned her lungs, and then I addressed the doctor.

"Tie my tubes," I said with all the authority I could muster.

"Have you discussed this?" The doctor looked at Number One.

"They're mine, not his. Tie them!" I demanded. I wasn't sure exactly why, I just knew I wanted it done, and soon. Maybe my command was a feminist battle cry. Or maybe a rejection of the cultural belief that women should have as many children as possible. My tubes were just a liability. Or maybe I was tired of the pain endemic to being a woman in a body. What I do know is this: I couldn't control what happened to my body while I was pregnant, and I can't control how my kids turn out. The one thing I can control is never doing this again.

6

THE CLASSICS

While our customers had finally learned that Diwan wasn't a library, they still seemed to want us to be more than a bookstore. I recall an interaction with Dr. Medhat, one of our most abrasive, and endearing, regulars. You may remember him from Egypt Essentials, where his search for an ancient Egyptian title unleashed a tirade about Diwan's insufficient reverence for pharaonic times.

Today's outburst began with: "How can there be no ancient Egyptian titles in your Classics section?" Medhat's capacity for indignation never failed to impress me. Still, I admired his passion. "Where is *The Story of Sinuhe*?"

"Out of print," I replied.

"As Diwan, it's your duty to publish it. Instead of filling the section with surrogates!"

"Diwan is not a publishing house," I responded apologetically.

"And why not?" he prodded. "You should do for publishing what you've done for bookselling."

"Maybe you're right." I'd given up. With some people, it's wiser to agree rather than to continue a doomed conversation. His suggestion was something Hind, Nihal, and I had considered over the years. Hind was the one who finally put her foot down, citing an Egyptian popular saying: leave the bread to the baker. Diwan is a bookstore; we sell books. And in the last seven years, we'd opened four stores—Zamalek in 2002, Heliopolis in 2007, then Maadi in 2008, and now Cairo University in 2009.

Despite seven years of similar interactions with Dr. Medhat, I was always caught slightly off guard by his on-slaughts. He had a righteous devotion to ancient Egypt, so of course our Classics section was a target of particular criticism.

"Dr. Medhat, I've tried to stock this section with time-less literature worthy of rereading."

"My dear, I'm sure you're familiar with Calvino's article about the virtues of revisiting the classics in one's mature years. He reminds us that great books incite rereading not because they root us in the past but because they speak to our present."

"Isn't that subjective?"

"No. Most books are like people. They live and they die. But the classics are immortal. I can see you've included the obvious titles of the Western canon," he said as he surveyed the shelves. His fingers ran across the spines of *Gilgamesh*, the *Iliad*, the *Odyssey*, the *Aeneid*, *The Canterbury Tales*. "And a few of our Eastern epics." He paused, studying one book. "The *Arabian Nights*! Seriously? Your shelves have power. Use it wisely."

"I am, Dr. Medhat, I am."

I'd never considered the *Arabian Nights*' place on Diwan's shelves controversial. I'd never imagined that it wasn't a clas-sic. Its contents clashed with the prevailing winds of con-servatism blowing through Egypt. But all of us—customers, booksellers, readers, and used-book dealers—had our own personal associations with the book. These associations gave it a life well beyond itself, illustrating Calvino's assertions perfectly.

What makes a book a classic? Gossipy, lowbrow literature in its time might become essential literature in the next, like Dickens. Spy thrillers, like Ian Fleming's, are published today as "classics." Who decides what literature is timeless? Some great works are forgotten or destroyed, and then later rediscovered in eras more amenable to their ideas and aesthetics. Some books speak to their moment but not to any future—successful and quickly forgotten. Who remembers Sully Prudhomme, the first winner of the Nobel Prize for literature?

As a child, I cherished the *Arabian Nights*. Most readers will be familiar with the book: a collection of Middle Eastern folktales, compiled during the golden age of Islam, *Alf Layla w Layla* in Arabic, meaning *One Thousand and One Nights*. The tales, held together by a frame story, originate in medieval Persian, Arabic, Indian, and Greek folklore and literature dating as far back as the tenth century. In the frame story, two kings, Shahrayar and Shahzaman, discover the infidelities of their queens and vow to exact revenge on womankind. In order to never be cuckolded again, Shahrayar marries a different virgin every night, deflowers her, and then beheads her the following morning. As you'll recall, one woman, Scheherazade, the vizier's daughter, puts an end to this bloodbath, outsmarting the king by telling stories that end each night in a cliffhanger, keeping the king from killing her, at least until the following evening. One thousand and one nights later, the king pardons Scheherazade, and they live happily ever after.

Fatma, my childhood nanny turned family cook, was a skilled storyteller. Though she couldn't read, she had memorized many of Scheherazade's tales. As a child, I could fall asleep only after an installment of the adventures of Sinbad the Sailor, Ali Baba, or Aladdin. In those years, every night of the holy month, a program called *Fawazeer Ramadan* aired on television. In 1985, the theme of the series was *One Thousand and One Nights*, and of course, I was hooked. The star, Sherihan, would perform Western and belly dance routines before presenting a nightly riddle. Her soundtrack was Rimsky-Korsakov's symphonic suite *Scheherazade*, intermingled with Egyptian folk tunes. I've written this book with that suite and Umm Kulthum's hour-long love song *Alf Layla w Layla* playing on repeat.

In short, I was obsessed. Scheherazade was my heroine. I promised myself that if I had a daughter, I would name her Scheherazade. I admired the character's authority and cunning. When I was pregnant with my first daughter, everyone—Number One, Faiza, Hind—tried to dissuade me from giving her such an esoteric name. I settled instead for Zein. A year later, I was pregnant again. I called my second child Layla.

But selling the book at Diwan was no simple task. We'd just opened our newest branch, a large shop inside Cairo University, when a student requested it. I listened as Mahmoud, a new hire, said we were out of stock. I knew this wasn't true, because I knew every shelf intimately. I looked on from one of the café tables that dotted the store. Each time we'd opened a new branch, Hind, Nihal, and I would spend our days there keeping tabs on our staff, and, just as important, getting to know the habits and needs of our new customers. And Cairo University wasn't just another store. Its setting was a utopian symbol of accessible education. Founded in 1908, the school was the result of Egyptian intellectuals lobbying and fundraising for a secular, modern, independent institution, the first of its kind. With the help of an endowment from Princess Fatma Ismail, the daughter of the ruler Khedive Ismail, the university opened, at first, to men, and later, to women.

The new store represented a huge ambition of mine, a dream achieved. We'd created our flagship shop to address a cultural deficit, but it catered to the literary elite. Our next two branches, Heliopolis and Maadi, were both located in wealthy urban areas where the upper and middle classes lived and shopped. We targeted adults with disposable incomes like ourselves. And in doing so, we'd neglected a huge subset of the Egyptian population: young people across different social strata. Diwan needed to be affordable, accessible, and well curated in order to succeed with younger generations. We needed to start a relationship where there hadn't been one.

That new relationship was riddled with contradictions. In honor of the store opening, Minou had designed a bag with an image of the school's iconic dome, surrounded by inspirational words in Arabic and English calligraphies. The irony was that the cost of producing one of those bags was greater than the margin on the average transaction at the campus branch, where students mainly bought café items and low-cost stationery. When they bought books, they were the cheapest paperbacks available. With every transaction, with every bag, we were losing money. Hind and Nihal suggested we stop giving out the bags, except with larger purchases. I refused. Behind my refusal was the fear that Diwan would have to change, to become a watered-down version of herself to survive in this new setting. If the thought was unsavory—upper-class neighborhoods got the real deal,

while lower-class ones got the knockoff—its logical extension was even more so: Diwan, and the culture of reading
it stood for, was a class-based pursuit that flourished only
among those who could afford it. I recalled the conversation with the journalist early on, who'd predicted the failure of our venture before we'd even begun: "People in Egypt
don't read anymore." If our profitable stores had to com-
pensate for their less successful counterparts, Diwan would
become a philanthropy, not a business. Minou warned me
that we were expanding too fast. I told her to shut the fuck
up. What was done was done.

The student who'd requested the *Nights* turned to leave.
As she made her way to the door, I intercepted her, introduced myself, wrote down her details, and promised that
Diwan would be in touch. I watched as she left the store
to rejoin her friends in the large courtyard, where we'd
hung two huge murals by Minou. I was proud of the outdoor space, which Nihal had designed: bright yellow tables
crowded by black chairs seemed invitingly haphazard. Unlike the flagship café chairs, which Hind insisted had to dis-
courage lingering, these were actually comfortable.

I turned back to confront Mahmoud.

"*Alf Layla w Layla* is in stock. It's right there."

"I'm sorry for the oversight. I must not have noticed it."

"You're observant as a hawk."

"I'm a good Muslim."

"And I'm a good bookseller."

"You shouldn't sell it."

"You shouldn't lie."

"You know they want to ban it. I agree with them. It has
things in it that are not part of our faith. Godless things."

I'd been closely following the case he referred to: A group of conservative lawyers, calling themselves Lawyers without Restrictions, had gone to court to remove a popular edition of the *Nights* published by a government entity and edited by the iconic author Gamal al-Ghitani. They wanted to replace it with a more sanitized edition. Like Mahmoud, they were outraged by the sexual language and the exaltation of wine, which they saw as a danger to Egyptian youth, a prelude to sin. He sympathized with them. I did not. Until the court's official ruling, I was committed to keeping that edition on my shelves.

"These stories were written down at a time when Islamic civilization was at its mightiest. It was the height of learning, conquest, and cultural output. Why can't you celebrate that?"

"How do you not see the pornography in it?" chastised Mahmoud.

"How do you *only* see pornography? And isn't there a difference between pornography and art?" I answered. "What you believe is your own business; your actions cost my business the sale of a book. So here's what you're going to do. Wait a day. Call the customer. Tell her you found it. You know I will check the system to make sure this transaction went through. If it hasn't, you know what happens next."

Mahmoud's attitude wasn't unique. Historically, the *Nights* engendered intense reactions from its conservative critics. Some thought moderate censorship was enough to conceal its lascivious subtext. Others banned it outright. Antoine Galland, the French orientalist, performed his own exorcism of the *Nights* when translating it into French for the first time in the early eighteenth century. The U.S. government banned it under the Comstock Law of 1873, which aimed to legislate public morality. It's still banned in Saudi Arabia.

In Egypt, *Alf Layla w Layla* was one of several battlefields where wars over identity and culture politics were fought. Throughout the last century, Egyptian governments have shuffled between secularism and conservatism with no clear or consistent ideology, deepening societal divisions. Debates and debacles ensued between incensed readers, governments, intellectuals, and the judiciary, unfurling over many decades. In 1985, a case was brought by another group of conservative lawyers against a publisher and two booksellers for producing and selling a racy version of *Alf Layla w Layla*. The judge ruled in favor of confiscating the print run and fining the three culprits five hundred Egyptian pounds each. Their crime: violating Egypt's anti-pornography laws and threatening the country's moral fabric. The judge pointed out that he wasn't banning all versions, just those that contained more than a hundred stories detailing sexual acts. Egypt's intellectuals expressed their outrage at the creation of a new dichotomy: Islamic versus pornographic. At the time, my father regularly read the work of the progressive journalist Anis Mansour, who protested the wave of Islamization sweeping through Egypt. My father understood that this wave was inevitable and unstoppable. The head of the Morals Department in the Ministry of the Interior proclaimed that the book posed a threat to Egypt's youth. He denied that the stories were part of our heritage, claiming instead that the book should be kept in museums. My mother, the eternal champion of all museums, found his myopia infuriating.

Other censorship dramas ensued and the courts moved on. The provocations of the *Nights*—namely, its metaphors, symbols, and abstractions of sex—were forgotten for a while.

Still, these images lurked in our minds, barely repressed. Books were always battlegrounds, even when the fights changed. Early objections had been on political and religious grounds. Then, sex itself became a target. No matter the named justification—sex, politics, religion—the conservative view tended to win. But in 2010, months after the exchange with the student, literature won. The ruling didn't mean that the book's placement in Diwan's Classics section went uncontested. Dr. Medhat's views had more supporters than I imagined.

Some of them, including certain Cairo University students, thought it wasn't literary enough to qualify as a classic. I would remind these customers that the tales had inspired troves of canonical literature shelved in the same section. Boccaccio's *Decameron*. Chaucer's *Canterbury Tales*. Marguerite de Navarre's *Heptameron*. In *Candide*, Voltaire refers back to Sindbad. Who can forget Tennyson's poem "Recollections of the Arabian Nights"? Or Edgar Allan Poe's "The Thousand-and-Second Tale of Scheherazade"? It's hard to read Borges without hearing echoes. John Barth's novella *Dunyazadiad*. Salman Rushdie's *Midnight's Children*. Even Stephen King's *Misery*, in which the protagonist is forced to write a novel under threat of death, recalls Scheherazade's plight.

This impressive roster wasn't enough to persuade doubting customers of the book's merit. I began to research different editions of the *Nights*, tracking how it shifted, transformed, and found new permutations. I knew that I wasn't going to find these editions easily. The stories had been passed orally, with a fluidity that both ensured, and threatened, their survival across generations. I knew exactly where to start: with my favorite book dealer, Hag Mustafa Sadek. When I visited him at his market stall at Suur

El-Ezbekiya, he suggested I come by his brick-and-mortar shop some Friday after midday prayers. I waited for a suitable number of Fridays to pass after our conversation, to give him time to source the books. Hag Mustafa had inherited his family business, which included the bookshop and warehouse, and his stall, from his great-grandfather. Mustafa and his fellow book dealers, who all sold at Suur El-Ezbekiya, worked in the alternative market, the antithesis to the government-owned publishers and failing bookshops of the time. They had an informal, diffuse network that evaded regulation and oversight and was far more efficient than the broken system upheld by government bureaucracies. Mustafa and his colleagues could source anything for a price.

Hag Mustafa had honey-colored eyes and milk-white teeth. He was a jovial man, invariably dressed in a 1980s safari suit. He gave me the honorary title of *doktora*. I descended the steep staircase into his shop, a cavern piled with books. A few were placed on shelves, but most were piled on the ground, in wobbly columns labeled with stray slips of paper. As usual, he offered me a cup of dense Turkish coffee. His delight was apparent as he sifted through the stacks on his desk for my prize. Finally, he seized a stained and weathered cardboard book perforated with holes. I knew what it was immediately: a rare 1892 edition of *Alf Layla w Layla*, published by Matba'at Bulaq, Egypt's first printing press, which was established by Muhammad Ali in 1820. Hag Mustafa knew treasure when he saw it. "This is a piece of history. The holes don't change that."

"Hag, you are a master!" Usually, I carefully measured my reactions around Mustafa, since I knew he studied the expressions of his clients to get them to shell out higher sums. But he was a seasoned dealer, and not even my most convincing performances muddled his instincts. And this time, I was too thrilled to compose myself.

"Just put it in the freezer. It will kill any remaining bookworms," said Mustafa. "Now, we negotiate. But be gentle." He was playing the prey, knowing full well he was the predator.

Mustafa's Matba'at Bulaq edition begins with the juxtaposition of faith and sex, one potential cause for conservative animosity. The opening verses invoke Allah, as the Western poets might invoke God. Allah's name sits squarely beside the impressive catalog of sexuality, eros, and adultery. The collection transgresses boundaries of race, class, and decorum. Still, many of the underlying ideas are normative and conventional, such as the cliché of female sexuality as a threat. Throughout the text, female desire must be controlled, harnessed, used as a tool for male pleasure. Pious men, virtuous women, brave warriors, virgins, demons, and harlots all meet ends suited to their deeds. Some modern versions rely upon stilted euphemisms, attempting to evade the censorship that the more debauched earlier texts faced. In these editions, the language of sex is cleansed of anything carnal. Physical encounters are rendered impersonally. Postcoitus, lovers resume their dealings as though they had exchanged polite salutations rather than bodily fluids. Nothing is real: it is metaphor, allegory, fantasy. Still, even these purified editions incite pushback from conservative commentators. They are guilty by association.

My next stop after Hag Mustafa was Hag Madbuli, newspaper seller turned bookseller turned publisher. The illustrious entrepreneur managed his relationship with government censorship masterfully. He'd been around forever.

My mother recalled seeing him on the beaches of Alexandria's Montaza each summer in the 1960s, wearing a white galabeya and beige overcoat. Clutching a bundle of books held together by a leather strap, he'd shout, "Livres nouveaux!" Later, he'd abandoned his father's wooden newspaper kiosk and opened a shop on Talaat Harb Square, in Cairo, with his brother. Even though he was illiterate, he was one of the shrewdest men in the business. He began his publishing activities in the late 1970s by enlisting the help of students who studied foreign languages. In exchange for store credit, they translated texts for him, which he'd then publish and sell at bargain prices. When I was a college student in the 1990s, he was my point of entry into forbidden literature. In between classes, I'd leave campus, cross Tahrir Square, and walk down Talaat Harb Street to his shop. Everyone knew that if you couldn't find a book, Hag Madbuli had it. From him, I bought the works of Egyptian feminists like Nawal El Saadawi, along with most other banned titles of the moment. It was rumored that even during the notorious 1985 court case, Hag Madbuli sold copies of *Alf Layla w Layla*. Later, he supplied Diwan with books he published. He was accustomed to Amir's witty banter and large orders. This time, my visit, and my singular quest, surprised him. Still, he delivered. I emerged from his shop triumphant, with an unexpurgated Arabic version wrapped in a black plastic bag, like someone hiding sanitary products while leaving the pharmacy.

That edition contained another key to the controversy: it mixed Fus'ha, classical Arabic, and 'Amiyya, colloquial Arabic. "Proper" classics could only be in Fus'ha, the language of the Koran. And yet here, the sexual passages in vernacular speech intermingled with didactic utterances in Fus'ha. Even though the alignment of "higher" language to noble actions and "lower" language to earthly acts was clearly demarcated, they shared a space, which was too close for comfort for some.

Other readers, especially young readers, knew the stories from more commercial adaptations, like the Disneyfied version of *Aladdin*. *Alf Layla w Layla*, in its modern iterations, had followed two parallel trajectories: children's literature and adult with a capital A literature. This polarization further entrenched people's assumptions. It was either suitable for children or unsuitable for mass consumption.

A different Egyptian epic, *al-Seera al-Hilaliya*, had a more prestigious place in our cultural imagination, even though its origins aren't much different than those of *Alf Layla w Layla*. This sweeping poem of love, war, and heroism was only recently published, despite having entertained Egyptians for the last six centuries. Its stories have traditionally been passed on orally by bardic figures, who meandered through the villages of Upper and Lower Egypt accompanying their tales with the *rababa*, a two-stringed lyre made of wood. Sometimes the *Seera* took up to seven months to narrate in its entirety. These storytellers, who learned their craft from their fathers and grandfathers, adjusted their tales to their audiences. Each lyric ended very differently depending on whether it was narrated east or west of the Nile. *Al-Seera al-Hilaliya* survives in part because of its accessibility and inclusivity—the entire community can listen to it. In all the versions I've encountered, there are no sex scenes.

In some ways, the *Seera* is understood as the Egyptian counterpart to the *Iliad* and the *Odyssey*. Perhaps this is due to subject matter. Homer, like the anonymous storytellers of the *Seera*, tells great chronicles of war and power. Of course, anyone who's read the *Iliad* knows that private griefs and marriage plots also abound. And the *Odyssey* has its own allegiance to the heart, as in Penelope's steadfast loyalty in her husband's absence, or Odysseus's affair with the glorious nymph Calypso. In contrast, the *Arabian Nights* is perceived as a seductive, if lowbrow, collection of fantastic tales. I think the two are not so different after all. Penelope's cunning, as she weaves a burial shroud for her husband's father and then secretly unravels it nightly, resembles Scheherazade's, both women delaying the manic pursuit of hungry men by spinning yarns.

The *Nights'* salacious reputation overshadows all its other qualities. For conservative critics, its erotic subject matter betrays the lowest human impulses. Others oversexualize it for different ends. I learned this one evening, when I stopped by Zamalek on my way home from visiting Heliopolis and Maadi. I wandered through the shelves, remembering the simple happiness of stacking and sorting in our early days. It was a form of meditation, another thing I no longer had time for. With each new branch, Hind, Nihal, and I faced the predicament of a parent with a newborn: how to divide our time and attention equitably among our growing family. We noticed a pattern. New stores lessened the sales of existing stores, without ever surpassing them. Older stores, left unattended, began to act out: displays, staff performance, and overall management slid into disorder. Even though we made a concerted effort to divide ourselves between Zamalek, Heliopolis, Maadi, Cairo University, and the stalls in the Carrefour City Centre Malls in Maadi and now Alexandria, to support and monitor our staff, striking a balance was impossible. Staff in older stores began to complain that new releases were being diverted to new stores. New stores complained that their sales were low because of insufficient stock. Everyone believed that they were victims in an unfair system that favored their rivals. No one took responsibility, or considered the surrounding economic landscape.

Still, the overall trajectory of sales was on an incline. The system functioned because we poured ourselves into it. The moment we stopped, or neglected one location even briefly, things yielded to the downward pull of gravity with shocking speed. Of course, being shit with numbers, it took me a long time to figure out that the problem was in the very nature of how we ran Diwan. A labor-intensive, high-quality operation that cut no corners demanded exorbitant overheads. Those overheads increased at a rate that would never match sales.

As I stood on Zamalek's shop floor surveying the stacks of books on the display tables, a distinguished-looking older gentleman approached me to ask for my assistance. He was dressed in a white *taub*, the long garment worn by Gulf Arabs, and a red-and-white head scarf, his dignified affect concealing his coarse attempt at youthfulness. He asked me for new releases in Arabic. I made a few recommendations, then enlisted the help of Ahmed, my favorite and most knowledgeable customer-service staff member, who now shuffled between the stores to train new hires. I retreated to my stacking, and after a while, the gentleman returned to ask me what my favorite Arabic classic was. Without thinking, I answered, *"Alf Layla w Layla."* He asked Ahmed to add it to his pile.

"You Egyptian women are a force to be reckoned with. Ahmed tells me you're one of the owners of Diwan."

"I am."

"A venture like this can't be easy."

"It has its moments."

"One day the women of my country will be like the women of yours."

"I'm sure. Enjoy the rest of your visit. And please let me know if Ahmed or I can be of any assistance." I returned to my task. After the gentleman left with his books, Ahmed walked over to me carrying a piece of paper.

"He asked me to give you this." He handed me the paper with some hesitation. I thanked him. He waited for me to read it. Was it a complaint? I opened the slip. It had four digits with a word scribbled above them in Arabic. Ahmed, who was quite tall, had a view of the note from above. I stared at the erratic handwriting, trying to decipher it.

"It's his hotel and room number," mumbled Ahmed. I felt a prickling in my scalp. Ahmed put both palms up in a calming gesture.

"Ibn el kalb el wisikh el wati," I hissed. I tore the paper to shreds. "If your colleagues on the shift ask, he was sending his compliments."

"Of course," said Ahmed, eyes on the ground.

That evening, I sat in the car on the way home in a daze, staring into the chaos of the traffic. Samir, undeterred by my unresponsiveness, chattered away, happily summarizing events and observations from his day. I replayed my dialogue with the gentleman in my head. Something in my manner must have encouraged him. Citing *Alf Layla w Layla* as one of my favorite books was a mistake. It probably had some double meaning. It was easier to blame myself than to try to understand such a presumptuous gesture. He must do this regularly: walk into a shop and leave his room number, believing himself irresistible. His entitlement infuriated me. I especially hated that he hadn't given me a chance to respond, except in my own head.

Around this time, I'd begun to suspect that Diwan had developed an independent personality outside of Hind's, Nihal's, and my plans for her. I know it sounds crazy, but I really believed that she had a mind of her own, one that could decide to accept or reject our ideas. She had trouble with our digital innovations. We built a website for her, and that worked well enough. But then we tried to design apps, and sell e-books, and we failed miserably. We weren't being true to the project, or to our (very technologically challenged) selves: we were brick-and-mortar, paper-and-ink, analog people. Ten years ago, industry experts predicted the death of bound physical books. Today, the same experts celebrate the comeback of independent booksellers. Even though everything except for the book itself, from production to retail, has become electronic, paper and ink remain.

These shelves have power. Use it wisely. Dr. Medhat's command from our last interaction propelled me to look at Hind's Classics section. While mine was dominated by epics spanning the ages, hers mostly featured poetry. Her collection ranged across centuries, from pre-Islamic *Jahiliyya*, to the early Islamic period, through to the golden age of Islam (the eighth to the fourteenth centuries), a period that overlapped with Europe's Dark Ages. I asked her why she included hardly any classics written in prose.

"This isn't an exhaustive catalog of the Islamic civilization's greatest hits. There was prose, sure, in the form of treatises and tracts. But those were mainly scientific, rather than literary, works." She continued to the next shelf. "Then you had the Egyptian literary renaissance of the 1800s, when translation to and from Arabic was rampant. And by the end of the nineteenth century, Arabic printing presses were taking off, catering to wider audiences and tastes. Indigenous traditions mixed with new Western forms, like drama and the novel." Her hands moved along the shelf. "There's another surge of poetry in the late nineteenth century, led by Ahmed Shawki, Prince of Poets, who epitomized the neoclassical age . . ."

"Poetry's not my thing." I gestured to Hind to move along.

"It is. You get turned off by Fus'ha." Hind continued before I had the chance to protest. "You love Umm Kulthum's songs. The most brilliant poets of the twentieth century vied to write her lyrics. That's why people still remember the words, even though her songs are seventy-plus years old. It's poetry set to music."

During customer-service training, there was little need to review Hind's Classics section. Most of Diwan's staff had studied the Arab poets in school. The public school curriculum, from my father's time in the 1930s through the present, contains a great deal of Arabic poetry. Its strictness, its forms, and its measures illustrate the rules of grammar and syntax. Students have to memorize and quote hundreds of verses and contextualize them in textbook fashion. Independent opinions and personal interpretation are unwelcome. Poetry isn't an art, but an exercise and an education. In theory, this program promises to build appreciation for the language. In practice, it produces hostile students who, like Marianne Moore, dislike poetry.

In the latter half of the twentieth century, as conservative religious movements became more mainstream, subtle changes occurred in the school curriculum. Nonreligious courses integrated more Koranic phrases as exemplars of Arabic language. Arabic literature, endowed with more flexibility in expression and form, received less attention.

Fus'ha is the language of the Koran, and a dead language seldom spoken in day-to-day conversation. It's guarded, frozen in time, by Al-Azhar, one of the oldest Islamic universities in the world, founded in AD 970, the center of learning for Sunni Muslims. During the early twentieth century, Salama Musa, a journalist and an advocate of secularism and socialism, lobbied to change the official national language from Fus'ha (classical) to 'Amiyya (colloquial) Arabic. He wanted to make written language more accessible to the masses. His initiative even garnered support from members of the Arabic Language Institute, which was established in 1932 by royal decree in service of preserving and studying the language. Al-Azhar, eager to preserve the sanctity of language, and the source of its power, fought this initiative to the death.

Not all of Hind's classics were poetry. Her section also showcased the masters of twentieth-century Egyptian prose: Ihsan Abdelkoddous, Tawfik al-Hakim, Yahya Haqqi, Taha Hussein, Youssef Idris, Soheir al-Qalamawi, Naguib Mahfouz, Youssef al-Sebai, and Latifa al-Zayyat. As a university student, I'd read their novels and short stories, which were written in a looser version of classical Arabic. While the language was by no means vernacular, it was far less rigid— their departure from convention paved the way for future experimentation.

Some of these writers had come up in the very university where we were standing, like Taha Hussein (1889–1973). Born into a lower-middle-class family in 1889, he was the seventh of thirteen children. At a young age, he contracted an eye infection and was left blinded due to improper medical treatment. He was sent to a *kuttab*, a school where children learned reading, writing, and the Koran. He then went to Al-Azhar University, the theological institution, where he clashed with the conservative school administration. Despite being blind and poor, he was accepted into the recently opened Cairo University, where he received his first PhD and eventually became a teacher. Like Dr. Medhat, Hussein was a proponent of pharaonism, an ideology that extricated Egyptian from Arabic history, whose supporters believed that Egypt's true renaissance could only occur through reclaiming the country's pre-Islamic heritage. While he authored numerous novels, short stories, and essays, he was best known for his 1926 work of literary criticism, *On Pre-Islamic Poetry*, which subverted the prevailing ideas about poetry at the time and raised subtle questions about the Koran as historical text. Al-Azhar, his former school, lobbied for legal action. The public prosecutor, in deference to the cultural climate of tolerance, declined to do so. Hussein's book was temporarily banned until a modified version was published the following year, entitled *On Pre-Islamic Literature*. Hussein lost his post at Cairo University in 1931, but in 1950, he was appointed minister of education, where he advocated for free and accessible education for all. He was nominated for the Nobel Prize in literature from 1949 to 1965, fourteen different times.

History repeats itself with different consequences. Sixty-nine years later, in 1995, Nasr Hamid Abu Zayd, a Cairo University professor, published *Critique of Islamic Discourse*, angering some of his more conservative Islamic colleagues, one of whom denounced him in a sermon at 'Amr ibn Al-'As Mosque. Lawsuits accusing Abu Zayd of apostasy followed. After years of legal turmoil, he and his wife left Egypt and went into exile in Leiden. I met him in 1999 at an Oxford University conference appropriately called "Rethinking Islam." He asked if I was returning to Cairo after the visit. I nodded. "Tell her I miss her," he said. After enough time had elapsed and the case against him had been largely forgotten, he returned to his homeland, where he died in 2010. In a case of poetic injustice, he died the same year *Alf Layla w Layla* faced the possibility of a new legal ban.

Dr. Medhat was right. Books live and die, like languages. Literary classics remain inaccessible to most Egyptians. While translations of Arabic classics proliferate internationally, they have few readers in the Middle East, due to the levels of illiteracy and the inaccessibility of the language. They aren't rewritten in 'Amiyya. Our relationship to the past is fraught and often superficial, in part because our doors to history are locked. And I wasn't sure a bookstore, or even four bookstores, could open it.

"This is just shameful!"

"Excuse me?" I turned, only to be met by Doktora Ibtisam, one of Diwan's most distasteful clients, who had migrated from Zamalek to the branch at Cairo University, where she was a professor. Her name in classical Arabic means "smile," which she never did and never inspired anyone else to do. "Doktora, what offends you today?" Hind asked with forced joviality.

"I can't believe how expensive your books are. Bookstores like yours make publishers greedy. They are pricing these books well beyond what anyone can afford. Not all readers have deep pockets like your Zamalek and Maadi devotees."

"I would have thought you, as a teacher of literature, would be in favor of investing in our literature and our culture."

"This isn't an investment. This is a rip-off. How do you promote reading if no one can afford your books?"

"I'm not as well-versed in Arabic literature as you," said Hind with genuine humility, "so I won't speak as a reader, but as a bookseller. When I first organized Zamalek's bookshelves, all we had were old editions that had been rotting away in warehouses. You remember: horrible paper, smudged ink, ugly covers, no spine, bound with rusty staples. Even though they cost a few Egyptian pounds, they weren't being read much. Now, less than ten years later, independent publishers see a wave of consumers who value quality and are willing to spend on it. Publishers bought available rights. They reprinted whatever was in the public domain. Look at the binding, the crisp type, the beautiful covers. Naguib Mahfouz's collected works have been released in multiple volumes, each one a wonderful contribution to any library. The masters aren't just being read, they are being cherished, revisited, and passed on to future generations. The investment in quality isn't deterring people from reading or buying these books. How many bookstores have opened since Diwan? How many new publishing houses?"

"Well, I want a discount on this book." She pointed to a recently released volume of Sufi poetry.

"As you know, it is against Diwan's policy to give discounts. However, I would suggest you try a library."

———

In the early 2000s, as existing publishing houses were expanding and new ones were building their lists, they moved beyond reprints and began releasing a greater variety of modern Arabic literature. People took renewed interest in Egyptian writers, many of whom had gained recognition in the eighties and nineties but only recently got their full due: Ibrahim Abdelmeguid, Radwa Ashour, Ibrahim Aslan, Salwa Bakr, Gamal al-Ghitani, Sonallah Ibrahim, Mohamed Mansi Qandil, Edwar al-Kharrat, Abdel-Hakim Qasim, and Bahaa Taher, to name but a few. Not satisfied with what was Egyptian and locally available, Hind had researched and stocked other critically acclaimed Arab authors, like Hoda Barakat (Lebanon), Mohamed Choukri (Morocco), Rabee Jaber (Lebanon), Sahar Khalifeh (Palestine), Abdelrahman Munif (Saudi Arabia), and Tayeb Salih (Sudan), who made it onto our bestseller lists. Before Diwan, these books were only available to Egyptian readers during the Cairo International Book Fair, when Arab publishers showcased their best-selling authors. Otherwise, they'd been trapped under the rubble of failed distribution channels. Hind found their publishers and imported from all over the Arab world. I was proud of her, and a bit jealous. I told myself that I'd find the English translations of her novels. She didn't share my competitive streak, caring mostly about introducing worthy readers to worthy writers.

Less than two years after opening, with minuscule book sales and rising rents and overheads, we were forced to close our Cairo University store. There must have been some truth to Doktora Ibtisam's grievances. My utopian vision for the location had met the cruelty of reality: students just wanted a place to hang out. Our café outsold our bookshop.

Hind always said that we had to go big or go home. Now, we had to go home. On departure day, stoic Nihal oversaw a team of maintenance staff as they packed books into cardboard boxes and dismantled shelves, lighting, and the café section. They would be stored and then repurposed in our next branch, our next attempt. Once we'd erased Diwan from the premises, Nihal handed over the keys to the campus administration. I couldn't even watch. She reminded me that knowledge was power, that we'd learned from our mistakes. The insights into what people want and don't want would carry forward. I told her that this had been a costly lesson.

Hind encouraged me to take a step back. I looked at the basic facts, the bigger picture. I reminded myself that we'd launched Diwan in a culture that had stopped reading. Our education system had emphasized rote memorization and discouraged freedom of thought. Disposable incomes, if people had them, didn't go toward books. Those who could afford to, like Hind and I, went to foreign-language schools that severed students from their native languages. Readers were alienated at every turn. Cultural output had been in a state of atrophy. And yet against all odds, change came about. Glimmers of hope.

Our flagship had become a Zamalek landmark. Heliopolis was doing steady business. Maadi was floundering a bit, but I knew that failure was a natural and necessary aspect of every experiment. Our stalls in the Carrefour City Centre Malls were reliably profitable. We were expanding to tourist destinations: the Cairo Marriott Hotel in Zamalek and Senzo Mall in Hurghada on the Red Sea. In the summer months, when Egyptians migrated to the coast, Diwan followed them with a seasonal branch on the Mediterranean coast. Maybe not all was lost.

Then, we drifted from the black into the unfamiliar red. We were in the throes of a global recession. I knew I was part of an international economy: even though I couldn't visibly see it, I witnessed its impact on our sales. Faced with diminished incomes, people grew anxious about the future and strove to preserve whatever resources they had. Leisure budgets were being funneled into emergency savings accounts and monthly bills. We sought new revenue streams to offset anemic sales. Cairo is a city that delivers: pharmacies, grocers, butchers, even McDonald's. Deliverymen double as personal shoppers: picking up a pack of cigarettes or something from a neighboring shop en route. I decided to launch a delivery service for our stores. Minou marked the occasion by designing a new bag with matching bookmarks. To advertise the initiative while the endless paperwork was being processed, I displayed in the window of Zamalek one of the delivery motorbikes that Minou had printed with her designs.

We started looking for corners to cut. The Diwan bags. It was becoming inescapably clear that we could no longer afford to produce them and give them out for free. I couldn't bear the thought of losing another of these simple pleasures in service to the bottom line. Later, when I finally broached the subject with Minou, she told me that canceling the bags would be a mistake I'd spend years regretting. I did it anyway, and I told her to fuck off. She was right, as usual. To this day, Minou has never forgiven me, and I have never forgiven myself. In my mind, the growth of Diwan was linked to the brand, and I worried that ceasing production of the bags signaled retreat. Our bags traveled everywhere; their high quality ensured that they outlived the things they carried.

They had become classics in their own right. As the *Nights* had taught me, not all classics survive, and those that do sometimes undergo a reincarnation that remakes their very essence. I watched as Diwan transformed: from something small enough to control to something far more unwieldy. Cairo University was the first store we lost, but it wouldn't be the last. Still, I knew we'd survive, if only through remaking ourselves.

"Dr. Medhat, I've been thinking about what you said," I tried to interject.

"At least your sister has the sense not to include *Alf Layla w Layla*." He walked off, fuming.

"Don't worry. He'll be back," said Ahmed, arms full of stacks of books, as he watched Dr. Medhat turn the corner into the cashier section of the Zamalek store, disappearing from view.

7

ART AND DESIGN

"This might surprise you, but *The Fireplace Book* is one of my bestselling titles in the Middle East," Stephen, a sales representative for the art publisher Thames & Hudson, said.

"This is one of the hottest regions in the world. Why the fuck would anyone stock—or buy—a book about fireplaces?" I scoffed.

"Haven't you sold enough books by now to know that you're selling far more than books?" He gestured around us, as if enlisting testimony from the books. We were standing in the middle of the Art and Design section of Diwan in Mohandiseen, our newest location. "You are selling an image, an aspirational lifestyle, a parallel reality."

We'd created Art and Design to group together books about aesthetics, which were larger in size than our standard fiction and nonfiction fare. But the new category quickly splintered into subsections, including art and artists, architecture, interiors, design, and photography. This was a far cry from Diwan's early days, when we sold only a few locally produced English- and Arabic-language art and design books, and every one of them focused on ancient Egyptian and Islamic heritage. These sold quite well, probably due to their traditional subject matter; we'd kept them in Egypt Essentials. The new Art and Design section was concurrent with growing global interest in art from the region. More modern art galleries had begun to open across Cairo. Sotheby's and Christie's set up shop in Dubai and began seasonal auctions of Near and Middle Eastern art, strengthening the market. Private collectors built private collections. A range of books chronicling contemporary Egyptian and Arab art and artists came out. Collectors bought books to contextualize their acquisitions. Egyptians found a new source of national pride beyond the works of Egyptian antiquity. This groundswell, and the increased demand it fueled, merited sections in both the Arabic and the English parts of Diwan's bookstores.

Alongside these contemporary movements, there was also an influx of photographic books, with images from late-nineteenth- to early-twentieth-century Egypt, before the 1952 revolution that ended the monarchy. Despite the massive political turmoil of colonialism and two world wars that marked the period, the photographs are surprisingly tranquil. Streets are clean and wide, punctuated by the occasional horse-drawn carriage or automobile. Images of Cairo's downtown, modeled on Paris, accentuate the belle epoque buildings and ornate façades. The people in the images are groomed and decorous. While I could see what the images concealed—the tumult and mess of life, the poverty and severe class hierarchies—I found the photographs comforting. They reminded me of the Egypt of my parents' stories, the distant place where they grew up. I began collecting these books.

Coffee-table books are all inherently decorative. Their buyers have leisure time, hours to peruse images and host guests. But the books also have an everyday quality. They live in and around us, like pieces of furniture. Their new-found popularity in Diwan's early years suggested a general shift in reading practices: books were no longer designed just for function, but for form. They were art objects in themselves.

"I'm accessorizing my home, and I'd like a selection of books on Egyptian art and design," I remember one customer saying to Hussein, our new customer-service hire, one afternoon. I was standing behind the cashier counter, cleaning the area below the till. This space was where damaged merchandise was stored and then forgotten, alongside lunch leftovers, key chains dangling protective evil eyes, and other staff belongings. The customer was a polished-looking woman in her thirties. She sported a Louis Vuitton monogrammed bag—with a matching scarf, of course.

"What era are you interested in?" asked Hussein. He'd been shadowing a number of seasoned customer-service staff across different Diwans, until being cleared to work in the freshly minted Mohandiseen store.

Mohandiseen, which translates to "engineers," was built on agricultural land offered by the government at discounted prices to the area's namesakes in the 1950s. Nearby neighborhoods followed similar schemes, creating districts for journalists, teachers, and doctors. These were occupations that benefited the community, especially valued after the 1952 revolution, which sought to establish an independent and modern Egypt. By the 1990s, following a dramatic population boom, these neighborhoods transformed; their original villas and spacious apartment blocks were torn down and replaced by densely packed concrete high-rises. Mohandiseen became especially congested: a labyrinth of shops, restaurants, and cafés, and a favorite destination for affluent Gulf Arabs summering in Cairo.

The neighborhood, known for its standstill traffic and nonexistent urban planning, was studded with towering concrete structures, jumbled shops, and ubiquitous banners and billboards. In short, it was charmless. We worried that Mohandiseen lacked the critical mass of sophisticated readers to call Diwan a third space, but we knew that it was a popular Arab tourist destination. With each location, we tried to learn from our triumphs, like Heliopolis, and our failures, like Cairo University. We tweaked our formula in the hopes of catering to our newly adopted community, or at the very least, entering into a dialogue with them. But we had a problem: our Zamalek flagship was an outlier, and had skewed all of our expectations. Heliopolis was three times the size of Zamalek, so we made the conservative estimate that it would generate twice the sales. To this day, Heliopolis has never fulfilled that expectation. We didn't realize that the combination of Zamalek's clientele—literary-minded Egyptians, tourists, embassy visitors, expats, and Francophiles—and its prime location on 26th of July Street would be impossible to replicate. Our expansion was built on a false premise, a stroke of luck. We didn't know it at the time, but we were trying to replicate a coincidence. We did know that the more we expanded, the higher our expenses, so we gambled on Mohandiseen's affluent residents to balance our budget. The woman in front of me certainly looked the part.

"My specs are bright colors, no black and brown spines— I'm not building the national library. I want a maximum height of thirty-five centimeters. But I also want to avoid visual monotony. I can stack a whole pile of them, and put a tray on top to make a side table." Hussein hesitated, obviously nonplussed. I interjected.

"Hussein, why don't you gather all the modern art books, and anything about Egypt from the last two hundred years. And maybe some ancient Egypt titles, but only the ones with happy and bright covers." I turned to the customer. "Would you like to join me in the café, to discuss the aesthetic you're interested in? I think we should start with the largest books at the bottom and place them horizontally. Anything you especially like that doesn't fit with the color scheme could be on the coffee table, and give you and your guests something to speak about." She gave me a smile that indicated she was pleased. I ventured further. "I know you asked specifically for Egyptian art and design books, but we do have a very special tome that someone with your taste would appreciate." I moved toward one of the displays for art and design books, an open wooden cuboid with multiple plexiglass dividers. I withdrew a massive book, *The World of Ornament*, published by Taschen, the German art book company. I exaggerated my struggle to lift the book to make its heft even more impressive. "We only import this for special clients. It weighs about thirteen pounds and stands quite tall, at a little over a foot and a half. It's a beautiful centerpiece. I promise you that very few people will have seen it before. It narrates the history of ornament, so if you're truly interested in design . . ." During training sessions, I would tell my staff that the surest way to sell a book was to put it in the reader's hands. I thrust this one into hers. She let out a little sigh of surprise. I could see the finish line. I laid out my final lure of bait. "It is a significant financial commitment, priced at one thousand two hundred and fifty Egyptian pounds, so please take your time considering it."

"It's well within my budget. I'll take it," she said with decisive gusto. "Do you have any books on interior design in Egypt?"

"Unfortunately, I can only think of two, which is surprising, given how many there are on Moroccan style and interiors. Somehow, contemporary Egyptian interiors haven't received the same degree of international interest." I brought her a pocket-sized book, also published by Taschen, called *Egypt Style*, which sold well because it was both cheap and beautiful, replete with lush photographs of interiors, an Egyptophile's dream. I handed it over.

"It's too small. It will get lost in the midst of all these other ones." She left it unopened on a nearby table. I placed the other title, *Egyptian Palaces and Villas*, in front of her, lifted the cover, and began turning the pages as I narrated, like a schoolteacher.

"I think you'll love this one. It features all the opulent palaces and country homes built since the time of Muhammad Ali, all the way through to Egypt's golden age as an international tourist destination. The aesthetic and cultural wealth of our country at the time of the Suez Canal, and the railways and cotton industries, was just magnificent. It's a must-have." She nodded in agreement.

"We forget how beautiful our country is. All this concrete gives our eyes amnesia." I remembered how people had reacted to our flagship store when they first walked in. Many assumed that our books would be overpriced, saying we'd spent too much on our interior. Others said that the design was distracting, that a bookstore shouldn't hide its function with useless decoration. Beauty was perceived as an unnecessary luxury. "My husband works in one of the leading stock brokerage companies. I've been telling him for years that we should collect art. He only recently began to agree with me, when he realized it was a good investment since his broker buddies are buying it, too."

"But for you, it's a passion?" I smiled. I appreciated her honesty.

She nodded. "I studied at the Faculty of Fine Arts in Zamalek. I dreamed of being a sculptor. Before that, I wanted to be an architect, but my father told me it was a man's profession." She paused. "But really, how many women can balance a demanding husband, his demanding children, and a career without going insane?"

"Hmm." I pivoted. "There aren't any women in the books you're buying. There was so much avant-garde design in Egypt from the thirties onward, but showing and championing female artists was still too radical." I wasn't sure whether I meant to be comforting or critical, only that I wanted to keep my personal life and views private.

She studied me. "Perhaps my father was right. Or unforgivably wrong."

"The problem today goes beyond the lack of women architects. It's the lack of architects, period. They've been replaced by *civil engineers*, designers with technical expertise but no aesthetic sense."

"And that's how we end up with neighborhoods like Mohandiseen," she lamented.

"Exactly. Now, please allow me to leave you in the very capable hands of Hussein," I said, as I led her toward the stacks of vibrant spines he had theatrically assembled on top of the display cases he'd cleared for this very purpose. He was a quick study. Nihal had hesitated in hiring him, because during his interview, he confessed that he knew nothing about books, coming from the hospitality industry.

Then he'd made a wild claim that he could tell what custom-ers wanted before he'd even spoken to them. Nihal decided he was full of shit. Hind agreed, and suggested that for this rea-son alone, we should try him out at Mohandiseen. This was new territory for Diwan, and we needed people who could think on their feet, who might succeed outside our usual (cultured, literary) customer base. The fact that, after several weeks of training, Hussein didn't know shit about books was less important than his affable affect and his ability to understand, and charm, a broad spectrum of people.

As I watched the woman leave the shop, I thought about what it was she'd wanted, and if she'd gotten it. Her precise specifications about color and measurement suggested that she'd bought the books as decorative furnishings, works of art. But her confession revealed that her interest was more than merely aesthetic: the books cataloged the private as-pirations she'd abandoned at her father's direction. It was obvious that her husband would use the new collection as a symbolic extension of his wealth and sophistication. I won-dered if he even knew about her early ambitions, if he'd ever asked.

There was one genre missing from Art and Design: the do-it-yourself home improvement book, which was very popu-lar with American publishers. The industry simply doesn't exist in Egypt. We hire handymen, carpenters, electricians, and plumbers, whose skills are passed down through gen-erations of families, or gained through community ap-prenticeships, to do these jobs. Several of the builders and contractors whom I worked with had begun their pro-fessional lives in one trade and then, through experience, picked up an awareness of the others, and then became successful contractors unhampered by guidelines or organizations that monitored or surveyed their work.

Their artistic counterparts are artisans, who go through similar processes of training. In the past, weavers, brass workers, coppersmiths, tentmakers, inlayers of mother-of-pearl, potters, and painters had formed an important social strata. Like handymen, masters passed on skills to apprentices, creating a closed system that ensured quality and knowledge control. Unlike more practical, marketable occupations, artisans are becoming extremely rare: unable to turn profits or compete with cheap imports, these makers, and their crafts, are dying out. Every so often, some group or initiative would attempt to rescue these artisans, setting up new shops designed for tourist traffic—but these efforts never succeeded in really changing the tides.

One joy of ordering and stocking Art and Design was sticking it to Hind. Our profit from one expensive, lavishly produced imported art book surpassed what we earned from two dozen Arabic books. Hind and I had staked our battlegrounds in our sections. The surrounding culture reinstated these disparities between Arabic and English in unsettling ways. Our local customer-service staff sold foreign books that, in some cases, cost more than their modest salaries. I started to see these asymmetries everywhere. Even Egyptian paper money embodied the binary of West and East. On one side, the numerical denomination is written in English, surrounded by illustrations of Khafra, builder of the medium-sized pyramid of Giza, Ramesses II on his war chariot, Horus's temple at Edfu, and Tutankhamun's funerary mask. On the other side, the Egyptian one, Arabic letters and numerals are surrounded by images of the mosques of Rifa'i, where the Shah of Iran is buried, Muhammad Ali, Ibn Tulun, and Sultan Hassan. This side was reductive, hiding non-Islamic and non-Arab Egypt from view.

While my staff and I inhabited the same city, our cities were not the same. Since the latter half of the twentieth century, the shift from rural to urban life has outpaced Cairo's ability to care for its citizens. As cities were marketed as the site of opportunity and government support, and massive urban migration followed, severe disparities between communities and classes became more and more accentuated. Aspirational images surrounded us. Billboards flanking Egypt's highways advertised concrete shoeboxes alongside plush palaces. Opposite realities grew side by side. *'Ashwa'iyat*, unplanned settlements that sprouted up on designated agricultural land, housed millions of hopeful transplants from the Egyptian countryside (where government services were less accessible and job opportunities more limited). Wealthy residents retreated from the growing slums into gated communities with swimming pools, gardens, and golf courses. Design books were marketed to the wealthy, providing images of beautiful worlds insulated from everything and everyone else. In the process, they made this lifestyle appear more organic, less alien. Elite classes were stratified into subsets, each making separate, but similar, aesthetic and commercial choices. The sales rep's claim about the popularity of *The Fireplace Book* comes to mind as an example of the strange fantasy I was actually selling. In the case of art and design books, they are the signposting of both outlook and aspiration. I could almost hear the books whispering to their loyal consumers.

I wondered how much the expensive books and affluent customers alienated and demoralized my less privileged coworkers. The books themselves belonged to a reality that my coworkers could hardly imagine, let alone inhabit. The options for social mobility were laughable. Theft was a constant at Diwan, from both clients and staff. Given the jarring discrepancies in standards of living, currencies, and commodities, I'm honestly surprised that we weren't stolen from more. It was much harder to forgive customers than my staff. The strangers always seemed remorseless when caught, unfailingly arguing that books were a basic human right, and therefore should be free for all, not unlike those early visitors' disappointment with Diwan's non-library status. We installed cameras and metal detectors and hired security guards. The customers improved their strategies for stealing, especially for multimedia items before the digital age made them obsolete. They would smuggle CDs and DVDs into the bathroom, slit the plastic covering on the side, remove the disc, and return the empty box innocuously to the shelves.

I also faced less literal forms of theft. Late one afternoon, I was speaking to my warehouse manager, Youssef, on the phone. I remember pleading with him: "Youssef, how are you progressing on the shipment? It's Wednesday and the books need to be on the shelves before the weekend."

"Ustazah, we are working very hard, but this is a six-ton shipment that requires both data entry and bar-coding."

"Just give me a percentage. How far?" Using a new surveillance program, I pulled up Youssef's computer screen on mine—even though we were in different buildings.

"We should be done by the middle of next week," he answered distractedly.

I hated being taken for a fool. It was thrilling to outsmart him. "Allow me to make a suggestion. It may help productivity. Stop playing online solitaire. It looks like you're losing, anyway." Silence. I went in with a left hook. "I'm docking your pay for wasting company time and funds—and for the shit example you set. You have until end of day tomorrow to finish the shipment. Feel free to work through the night." I hung up. I told myself that if my staff chose to withhold their work in favor of playing cards, I was allowed to steal their privacy, to ensure I received the labor I paid for.

A few hours after the incident, I was walking past the kitchen in the head office, where I found the data-entry team sulking, nursing their tea with uncharacteristically subdued voices. Omar, the IT manager and normally a permanent fixture of this group, was absent. I continued to his office, entered without knocking, and closed the door behind me. He stood up.

"There was trouble in the Garden of Eden this morning," I said.

"Ustazah, when I installed the spy software, you promised me you would not tell the staff."

"Omar, sometimes I have to play my hand. You haven't been burnt. They need you more than you need them." He looked on politely. I appreciated Omar's courteous manner as much as his software capabilities. He was a symmetrical young man who styled his jet-black curly hair with a sheen of gel, who always wore crisp black pants and ironed white shirts.

Later, Omar helped facilitate my transition from spy software to motion-activated webcams in the warehouse, whose feed automatically connected to my computer as well as to Hind's and Nihal's. They never looked. Employees suspected that I was watching, and they were right. I may have taken inspiration from the Nasser era to confront the legacy of the Nasser era. I remember hearing stories of

Nasser's state security officials dangling microphones from apartment balconies to overhear party guests' political sentiments. I became omnipresent in my determination to confront Nasser's socialist legacy—free education and state employment for all—gone amuck: the listless employee. Many Egyptians aspired to a government job, with its promise of shorter working hours, meager pay (which could be enhanced through more creative channels), and the guarantee of a job regardless of performance (Nasser's laws made it very difficult to fire government employees). Private companies, like Diwan, received bad press. While our pay was better, we demanded an eight-hour workday and measured output, and we fired those who didn't meet our standards. Egyptians were torn between the path of least resistance and uncharted territory, with its potential for greater gain.

Beginning in ancient times, the Nile provided water, food, and transportation. When the river overflowed, the fertile silt it left behind made farming effortless. Herodotus, the ancient Greek philosopher, had written, "Egypt is the gift of the Nile." Depending on where you stood, the Nile's abundance could be seen as modern Egypt's curse, perpetuating a culture of inaction.

When a customer spent a thousand Egyptian pounds at Diwan, their loyalty was rewarded with a one-hundred-pound gift voucher. But because of certain loopholes in this policy, Diwan was faced with a rotating band of thieves straight out of "Ali Baba," one of my favorite tales from the *Arabian Nights*. In it, Morgana, Ali Baba's shrewd slave, foils the plots of the thieves who are trying to kill her master for having uncovered their cave of riches. I had multiple Morganas.

Omar was my most steadfast accomplice, and his latest contraption captured surprisingly crisp footage. As the Nile waters flowed to fill its different tributaries, money moved through Diwan's branches. Maged and Omar regularly generated reports to monitor those movements. They'd flagged the Maadi branch for an unusually high number of gift voucher redemptions, which inexplicably took place during the quiet morning shift. I'd transferred Hany, a tentative and gentle cashier who worked that shift at Maadi, to the Heliopolis branch for further scrutiny. The next day, I visited the store under the guise of discussing the displays and checking the branch's overall appearance. When no one was looking, I quickly placed my new hidden-camera spy pen—a toy from Omar—at an angle on the shelves adjacent to the cashier. I asked Samir to engage his well-to-do cousin, an accountant in a multinational firm, for some undercover work that afternoon. I watched through the spy pen as Samir's cousin purchased the hefty *Star Wars Archives: 1977–1983*, priced at a little over one thousand Egyptian pounds. Lo and behold, Hany didn't offer him a gift voucher. After the cousin left, Hany scanned his surroundings, printed a voucher, attached it to the *Star Wars* receipt, converted it to cash, and slid the one-hundred-pound note down his navy-blue shirt, flattening it against his belly. After earlier incidents of theft, Nihal had begun sewing the pockets of uniform trousers shut before issuing them to staff.

Later that day, as I went to Maged's office, I glimpsed Hany waiting patiently outside. I ducked my head into my bag, fumbling for a distraction. My mouth was dry. We were family. But I knew the drill. I'd participated enough times. Maged will lay out the information in cheerful, buoyant tones, enlisting Hany in the investigation and feigning bewilderment. Omar will explain the numbers and strange coincidences with excessive jargon. Maged will then ask Hany if he has any knowledge that could shed light on the gift-voucher-redemption issue. Hany will appear horrified at this mere hint of wrongdoing, swear on his mother's honor, and fervently deny the claim. Maged will nod in agreement while pressing Play on the video footage. The hair on the nape of Hany's neck will rise.

Maged will give him two choices: The first will be to resign, signing a declaration that the company has fulfilled all its obligations toward him and that he will not file any labor complaint against it (a clause we'd added following previous cheeky thieves who'd done just that), and write a series of checks to the company, paying back an estimate of what was stolen. Or Hany could choose to let us call the police; they will take him to the police station, where he will be questioned and charged based on a confession he gives, either of his free will or after unorthodox persuasion. He will emerge a broken man, weighed down by the shame of what happened to him. His record will render him unemployable, and he will have a life of only more crime to look forward to.

Hany will offer meek resistance and beg for mercy. Maged will tell him this is mercy. Hany will ask to speak to the kindest lady of Diwan—Nihal. Maged will continue to berate him. Hany, exhausted, shaking, will sign the declaration. Omar will enjoy all the excitement. Samir, the world's most verbose driver and vocal critic of his employer, will struggle to keep his part in all the drama to himself. Maged will feel triumphant, but maybe frustrated at not having gone far enough. I will swallow the rust of my rage at this nation that has left its citizens few options for security and stability outside of theft. The Hanys that I have met, and employed, will never be able to save money, take out a mortgage (home financing formally began in 2001 and is still in its nascent stages), or piece together a decent life, even with years of hard work. They will hope for a pocket of concrete in which they can raise a family and live in debt. Faced with Hany's life trajectory, what would I have done? Hind and Nihal, certain of their own morality, were unwavering in their decisiveness to punish thieves. They knew that if their circumstances were the same, they would never steal. I began to realize, with some disappointment, that my clemency stemmed not from some inherent kindness but rather from a lack of confidence in my own moral fiber. What kind of an asshole do you have to be to prosecute Jean Valjean?

Outside, the asphalt steamed with heat. Samir leaned against the side of the car, merrily bantering with the porters sitting nearby, regal in white galabeyas. Upon seeing me emerge from the office building, he gestured to them that their conversation would resume on his return. Still eager to distance myself from Hany's plight, I locked my eyes on the passenger seat that awaited me, hoping that my paces were more measured than they felt.

"I saw Hany walk into the office. Did he sign, or call your bluff?" asked Samir, gripping the steering wheel of the car in anticipation.

"You should never look on the misery of others as entertainment."

"Yours or his? Everyone in the company knows that you'll never call the police. So, every thief takes his chances: if he gets caught, he pays it back." Samir pulled out of his spot, slipping the parking attendant a couple of pound notes.

"A thief should be punished, but sending him into the unjustness of our justice system is ending his life," I responded.

"If you're weak enough to steal, you deserve what's coming. You just feel guilty because you have money and he doesn't," Samir explained. We were driving to Sun City Mall, our newest location and the first in a mall. Before opening our earlier locations, we'd had months, sometimes even years, of debate. About neighborhoods, about cost, about brand, mission, responsibility. At this point, we'd resolved to go bigger (and not go home), so we didn't deliberate for nearly as long, despite the seriousness of the commitment. Malls were the future, whether we liked it or not, and Diwan had to be there. Besides, we were still trying to make ends meet, and we weren't succeeding. But there was always the hope that the next store would bridge the ever-widening gap.

I looked out at the rooftops, crowded with satellite dishes, air-conditioning compressors, and loose cables, as we inched down 6th October Bridge. The bridge, an elevated highway, is named for the date that Egypt crossed into occupied Sinai on Yom Kippur in 1973. Ironically, the bridge was conceived as an observatory for Egyptians to enjoy the view of Cairo's landmarks on their commutes: the Cairo Tower, the Nile, the Maspero Television Building (named after Gaston Maspero, the French Egyptologist), the Egyptian Museum, Cairo's railway station. Instead, we peered into the windows of homes and offices directly abutting the freeway, glimpsing the lives of people who'd never expected a bridge to be constructed in front of their kitchen sinks and cubicles. I was grateful for August's heat, which brought the annual exodus from Cairo to the crystal waters of the north coast. The city was empty, and I was free to rush through it. I didn't mind the weather. The relentless sun soothed me. As if he could hear my thoughts, Samir interjected, "When are you heading to the coast? I can't take this heat anymore." He blasted the air-conditioning.

"When I finish what I need to do," I responded, rolling down my windows.

"When the girls are older, their needs will overrule yours." He switched off the air-conditioning. "They are entitled to smell the sea breeze and eat fresca on the shore. You can't lock them up in an apartment all summer because of *your* work."

Samir drove Masri (Egyptian) style: straddling two lanes to prevent another car from overtaking him, emitting random bursts of honking to remind the road of his presence. I asked him to pick a lane. He suggested I do the same: focus on bookselling and leave the driving to him. We sped through the twenty-kilometer stretch of 6th October Bridge, continuing down the flyover, crossing the old tram tracks, until we reached Salah Salem Street. Gray clouds hovered above the city we left behind.

"The wife of the owner of the Baehler building is kicking out the kitsch shop a few doors down. The lease expires in a month and they can't pay the new rent. It's a good opportunity for Diwan." I didn't respond. "The shoe shiner who comes to the building has just retired and is giving his nephew the patch. Do you want to try him out?"

"There are no shoes in our house that need shining."

"Maybe one day there will be," quipped Samir, always hopeful. While he believed I was one of the few who could survive without a man, he constantly reminded me of his preference that the interim period between Number One and the onset of a new era with Number Two (whom I hadn't met yet at the time of this exchange) would be short. He cut off my attempts at silence like a tailor following the lines of his pattern. "He'll be looking for a part-time job. Can you use him as a night watchman for the Zamalek store? I hear 'am Abdu's wife is making him resign because she's fed up with him staying out all night." Samir chuckled.

"I don't shit where I eat, and neither should you." I put the radio on, hoping that this would bring an end to Samir's roster of real estate and employment opportunities. I didn't like inviting my home life into my business. But given Cairo's interconnectedness, my attempts at the separation of these worlds were futile. Hind, a silent realist, wasn't bothered by this diffusion of boundaries. Early on, Abbas, her personal driver, had four of his cousins working in Diwan, a number that grew exponentially over the years. Abbas is still Hind's driver, and is revered by our children. Samir and I parted ways a few years ago.

Cairo International Airport rose out of the Sahara on our left. Samir continued down al-Nasr Road, the last stretch of our journey. This was the border of the Cairo I knew and the frontier of the Cairo I didn't know. The new highways and ring roads challenged my limited sense of direction. Samir, happily aware of his growing indispensability, played up the tactical choices he was making to get me to my destination. As I looked at the endless desert in the distance, I had a familiar thought: in no time at all, this vacant expanse would be unrecognizable. I resented this extension of the city that was sweeping up sand dunes and spilling onto the surrounding desert: gated communities and palatial wedding-cake homes. Around us, suddenly, slabs of gray rose up into view: unfinished government-funded concrete shoeboxes for housing lower- and middle-income families. The green spaces were scraggly and brown. The desert was still asserting itself. My city was in survival mode, as it has been for the last few decades. Mubarak and his revolving cabinets had proved themselves unable to make plans or keep them. They were prone to ugliness, both moral and aesthetic.

Malls stood at the center of these crises. As Cairo's affluent classes withdrew to newly designed suburbs, malls emerged to cater to this new influx. The loud advertising of cost-efficient Carrefour market, with its endless shelves of identical produce, threatened the quiet dignity of small family-run shops and stalls. High streets became less essential. The deeper loss was the sense of community that these streets had once engendered. I thought about the relationship the youngest generation, growing up in gated communities and compounds, would have to their surroundings. I can't imagine cultivating a sense of civic duty and belonging from behind such high walls. I remember fondly how Hind and I as kids would accompany our parents to the different shops and stalls on 26th of July Street in Zamalek. I would watch as modest interactions blossomed into deep affinities. Vendors and customers *knew* one another, even without knowing one another.

Closing my eyes, I can still see 26th of July Street perfectly. On one corner of the uneven pavement, Magdy's stands displayed local and foreign newspapers and magazines held in place by clothespins. With one side of his checkered shirt hanging out of his trousers, Magdy spent mornings delivering papers on his bicycle. In his absence, he trusted that no one would steal from his stand, and no one ever did. The government-owned Al-Ahram Distribution Agency held a monopoly on the supply and distribution of all magazines and newspapers. They swindled Magdy by fudging the dates of returns; he mitigated his losses by spreading them across his clients. When questioned by my mother about our fluctuating monthly bills, Magdy would scratch the side of his nose with his long—but exquisitely filed—fingernail, and then explain that this was the will of government and God. My mother would rebuke him, promise to go elsewhere, and then she would pay the inflated bill. This exchange recurred at the end of every month.

Umm Hanafi squatted next to Magdy's stand. She was a proud *fellaha* with pearls for teeth and a back straighter than a palm tree. She was always clad in a pristine black galabeya, and a flowery head scarf was tucked behind her ears, tied at the nape of her neck. Dangling circular earrings pulled at her earlobes. The three green parallel lines running down her chin confirmed her Bedouin origins. Occasionally, there was a child suckling at her breast. Every morning, she walked for miles to get to Zamalek, woven wicker tray swaying on her head, to sell dozens of freshly baked loaves of baladi bread. Directed by my mother, we bought from her, not from the government-subsidized oven at the end of the street.

Madbouli, the fruit and vegetable seller, spilling out of the plastic armchair in the corner of his shop, was a permanent fixture. My father bought fruit and vegetables from him, constantly arguing over their quality; my mother's eyebrows rose and fell at his prices. When I was older and did the shopping for my own home, I sorted, smelled, and selected mangoes from the imposing pile at the front of his shop. He used to throw in a couple of overly ripe ones in retribution. By then, Madbouli had discarded his galabeya for trousers and shirts; they were less kind to his portly form. These shops and their owners occupied a big part of my childhood, and they are still there in one form or another. Magdy, missing a few more teeth, has an apprentice circling Zamalek's streets on his bicycle distributing newspapers. Umm Hanafi's patch of pavement is empty. Madbouli has been joined by his extended family in manning the shop. Farther down, a mobile phone shop replaced the bakery.

The simultaneous demise of the high street and rise of the mall should have caused its own revolution, an occasion for rethinking our streets and our expectations for civic space. Instead, Egyptians peacefully gave in to the call of the mall. Cinemas. Starbucks. McDonald's. Zara. Mango. Ice rinks. As public spaces were eroded, malls offered lavish, privatized replicas of plazas and parks. Families enjoyed a comfortable air-conditioned environment where they marveled at the prices of all the imported goods they couldn't afford. Unmarried couples relished a space where they could hold hands undisturbed, stare at windows of furniture shops, and share cheap sodas. Public bathrooms were regularly cleaned and stocked with soap and toilet paper, unlike anywhere else in Cairo. Ease and convenience are the defining conditions. But nobody stopped to think of the repercussions. The lack of intimate exchanges between shopkeepers and customers. The growing separation between where we live and where we invest. There is nothing in the mall worth holding on to. Even its perfection has an artificiality that makes it ugly.

When we arrived at Sun City, I got out of the car and asked Samir to wait for me in the parking lot. I couldn't handle the thought of him coming into the new Diwan, offering his unsolicited feedback on what we'd done and what we could've done better. I trod carefully on newly polished marble floors, scared to slip. Crystal air, fake palm trees, and sweeping staircases, under the trompe l'oeil dome, painted with a Renaissance knockoff of some impossibly blue sky, worked together to suspend reality. I spotted Diwan's familiar logo, located opposite the entrance to the cinema. I walked along the new shop façade, checking the glass for scuffs, reviewing the offerings of Arabic and English books in the window display. Inside, I saw Nihal with the new store manager, cashiers, and customer-service, café, and maintenance staff. I set aside my doubts, pushing the long chrome door handle, just like the one on the door in Zamalek. The air in the room smelled of potential, like a new car: the shelves were perfectly stacked, books on the display tables were neatly aligned, and the tills and the staff still had a freshness about them.

Nihal's kind eyes allayed the fears of new staff members, while her words expressed the gentle ruthlessness with which she managed people. Nihal pointed to the pile of folded clothes individually wrapped in plastic on the table next to her as she gave her spiel. "You will wear these at all times while conducting business for Diwan Bookstores, and you will behave according to our standards. Oh, and all uniforms are the same, regardless of rank." The manager frowned. The maintenance staff smiled. "Your position is on your name tag." When the room quieted down, Nihal continued: "The pockets of the trousers are sewn shut to avoid temptation, or false accusation. You can leave your personal belongings in your lockers when you change your clothes at the start of your shift."

Most employees lived in 'ashwa'iyat, settlements on the outskirts of the city. Through an illegal process, individual citizens seized agricultural land, building unlicensed residential properties. In an act of willful denial, the government didn't extend essential utilities, such as electricity, to these areas. Landlords stole electricity from nearby settlements or found ways to use generators. Once some time had elapsed and the arrangements became more permanent, the government was begrudgingly forced to accept what was. Residents and bureaucrats worked together to create a no-man's-land: not fully acknowledged or granted public services, but not under imminent threat of removal. Entire communities, housing millions of people living in subhuman conditions, were cramped on the edges like this.

"Cleanliness is akin to faith," Nihal went on. The men nodded in agreement. "We all know how hot it gets, how crowded the buses are, and how slow the traffic is. By the time you get here to start your shift, it is as if you have run a marathon. Diwan is our oasis, we have our ways of doing things and we keep a standard for ourselves, regardless of the outside world." I found relief in the familiarity of this performance, and in being part of the audience. Her eyes met mine. "I also want to highlight some more items from Diwan's employee handbook," she said, as she pulled out nail clippers from her handbag. "At Diwan, long fingernails are not tolerated because they don't fit with our image—especially the little finger." I heard whimpers. Most working-class men distinguished themselves from laborers by growing the nail of their pinkies, implying the impossibility of manual labor. Shuffling feet. Nihal sensed rebellion. "You represent Diwan. We have our way of doing things. We learn from one another. We don't force anything, we guide." She wore the demeanor of a mother pleading with her children. The nail clippers made their rounds between the men. Crisp clicking sounds continued in the background as Nihal listed her other demands.

My cue approached. Nihal had called me in for the final act of the orientation. As her soliloquy came to an end, she directed the men to me. I cleared my throat and I summarized myself: my name is Nadia, I am Nihal's partner, I am responsible for the divisions of finance, marketing, and English-book buying, and I am proud to be a member of Diwan's family.

"As Islam teaches us, work is one of the purest forms of worship," I told the room. "For this reason, we do not allow prayer on any of our premises. Should you wish to pray, find a mosque, and remember that time spent in prayer is deducted from your breaks. The company pays you for your time and effort. Wasting it is stealing from the hand that feeds you. And thieves will be prosecuted." The silence got heavier. Like confused children, the men turned their heads back to Nihal.

"Welcome to the family." She smiled.

8

SELF-HELP

Not all books are created equal; some are more equal than others. Even though Self-Help was the fastest-growing section of Diwan, I didn't read those books. I had always turned to literature to be challenged, to deepen my sense of self and the world. Self-help did the exact opposite: it explained nuance away. It prescribed. At least, that's what I thought at the time.

Up until Hind and I met Nihal, and the three of us opened Diwan, I'd never even touched a self-help book, let alone read one.

"If I drink the crap you put in my water, do you promise to stop pushing this bullshit on me?" I remember bartering with Nihal, as she gently slid a copy of James Redfield's *The Celestine Prophecy* across the table to me.

"How do you know it's bullshit if you haven't read it?" she responded with a half smile.

"I can smell it."

"Why go through life blinded by your own arrogance?"

"Why not? You do the same. Our sources may be different, but our arrogance is equal."

"How do you nourish your soul?" questioned Nihal, her tone full of pity.

"I work hard."

"I made spinach, apple, and raisin salad with a curry dressing for lunch today. Want some?" Nihal gushed, offering up the bowl.

"No, thanks. I'm on a diet." Even as I said this, I felt my resolve waver. I looked at the salad, its shiny film of dressing beckoning me.

"Don't succumb to the diet mentality. That's how you gain weight."

"Shut up! You sound like a fucking self-help book." I knew I was being a bitch. Nihal relied upon her remedies and solutions, wherever she found them. In homeopathic vials. In the cryptic clues left by angel cards. In the pages of the many self-help books she *insisted* Diwan stock. We settled into a pattern, in which Nihal would recommend purchasing some buzzy new self-help book for the stores. *The Power of Positive Thinking, The Power of Now, Awaken the Giant Within, You Can Heal Your Life, The Road Less Traveled, Chicken Soup for the Soul*—it didn't matter. I would scoff. She would continue, at regular intervals, to ask me whether I had ordered it. Finally, I would acquiesce. And then it would invariably sell extremely well. Demure Nihal would never acknowledge her victory directly.

"You should get all the other titles by these authors. They have such a loyal following," Nihal would propose innocently.

"Wouldn't that suggest that they aren't delivering on their promises? If one book didn't solve the problem, how could the next one claim to?"

"Truly dedicated readers never stop learning, even if it means approaching the same issue from different angles."

"Does it ever occur to you that these books are a con? In the pharmacy of the soul, could you be falling for the placebo effect?"

"I know why I like them. Do you know why you hate them?"

One of Nihal's greatest qualities is her light touch. I kept thinking of her question, which was really a challenge disguised as a question. Our stores in Zamalek, Heliopolis, Maadi, Mohandiseen, Alexandria Library, and even the newly opened Sun City Mall felt like shrines to self-help, proving Nihal's point. Only the Diwan inside Cairo Airport's duty-free shopping area had been spared the self-help torrent, since it was mostly comprised of Egypt Essentials, targeting travelers. No matter how much we expanded these sections, dividing them into subsections for relationships, diets, personal growth, healing, and spirituality, they never fully satisfied demand. For every new title and series, Nihal had a knowing smile. Hind chose not to weigh in, instead quietly hunting for any Arabic translations.

As sales skyrocketed, I was forced to face my distaste for the genre. I wanted to understand my customers' desires. I'd initially assumed my animosity toward self-help stemmed from snobbery: it didn't qualify as literature. But I felt a bit blinded, unable to see what others saw in these texts. I used to be less judgmental. I remember saying, "I don't care what you read, as long as you read." Now, I cared a lot.

I began looking into the origins of self-help texts. Samuel Smiles, a largely forgotten author, may be the ultimate originator of the modern-day genre. His story collection, *Self-Help*, which he (appropriately) self-published, details the lives of hardworking men (no women) who triumph over their circumstances. It was published in 1859, the same year as Charles Darwin's *On the Origin of Species*, and outsold every other book on the market except the Bible. That year, Smiles became an early celebrity, a guru of anti-materialism, the ironic father to a multibillion-dollar industry.

As I soon discovered, the genre significantly predates Smiles and is intimately related with, you guessed it, the ancient Egyptians. *Sebayt*, literally "instruction" or "teaching," was a genre of pharaonic wisdom literature. The oldest surviving self-help book is widely believed to be *The Maxims of Ptahhotep*, or *Instruction of Ptahhotep*, which was written somewhere between 2500 BC and 2400 BC and not discovered until the mid-1800s. Ptahhotep, a vizier during the rule of Pharaoh Isôsi of Upper and Lower Egypt, the penultimate ruler of the Fifth Dynasty, was an elderly man on the verge of retirement who was eager to pass his position on to his son. The king, not wishing to disappoint his loyal subject, hesitantly approved the succession, on the condition that his wise man pass his knowledge on to his inexperienced son. Ptahhotep wrote this guidance as a letter, extolling the virtues of silence, timing, and honesty, and discussing the importance of relationships and decorum. His rules were copied by scribes and shared broadly. His letter belonged to this burgeoning genre that directed readers to live according to Maat, the ancient Egyptian goddess who ruled the stars and the seasons, and also tempered the actions of mortals and deities alike. She personifies the concepts of truth, balance, harmony, law, morality, and justice (she reminds me of Nihal). I looked for collected sebayts to stock in Egypt Essentials because I wanted to claim sebayt as the ancestor of self-help.

In Egypt Essentials, we'd provided at least thirteen ways of looking at our country. In the case of self-help, I hoped that the establishment of its philosophical lineage might restore to it some of its lost sophistication and nuance. In my mind, the awareness of its illustrious past, which focused on the transfer of wisdom and the lofty aspiration of assisting readers in their pursuit of meaning, might help balance the cheapening onslaught of TV adaptations, ridiculous spin-offs, and soulless franchises that plagued the modern self-help-book market.

Advice on living well seemed to have been a central project of most civilizations, once they managed to survive ice ages and ferocious beasts. Ancient Greek texts peddled meditations, aphorisms, and maxims on eudaemonia, "the good life." From the fifth century BC to the Hellenistic period, Greek philosophers tackled issues pertaining to bettering the self in order to lead a worthier life. Plato emphasized man's obligation to the common good. Socrates advocated for questioning one's own existence. Aristotle believed that a virtuous person excels at being human. Zeno of Citium, the founder of Stoicism, suggested that we can live a virtuous life, a good life, by being in harmony with nature, with our surroundings. From highbrow to lowbrow, philosophy to self-help, the central concern of humans, once survival was guaranteed, was to thrive, to do and be better. Seeing the self-help genre as a continuation of this human quest began to attenuate my animosity toward it.

The mirror-of-princes genre, inspired by the writings of the ancient Greek historian Xenophon, told of the deeds of kings and notables for emulation, with a few cautionary tales. After the invention of the printing press, these texts found wider audiences. Baldassare Castiglione's *The Book of the Courtier* (1528) and Giovanni Della Casa's *Galateo* (1558) brought forth the era of savoir vivre books, which told people how to behave. Niccolò Machiavelli's infamous political philosophy treatise from 1513, *The Prince*, to this day sells very well in Diwan—in the Philosophy section.

Sun Tzu's *The Art of War*, an ancient Chinese military treatise written around 500 BC, became a bestseller among our
business books. I always wondered what made these books
popular at this particular time, in this particular corner
of the world. I read that Marcus Aurelius's *Meditations* was
a bestseller in contemporary China. The promise of agency
in these books must have been tantalizing to those of us
who felt helpless, whether politically or personally. The
ancient Romans transcribed multivalent self-help texts of
their own. Cicero, the translator of Greek philosophy into
Latin, and one of the most prolific authors of the age of
Julius Caesar, wrote *De Amicitia* (*On Friendship*), *De Senectute*
(*On Old Age*), and *De Officiis* (*On Duty*), advising Romans on
how to live and be in different stages and contexts in their
lives. These subjects are still pertinent. I worry about my
friendships, my responsibilities, and how to deal with myself and others as I grow older. I know other people share
these concerns because they buy books that promise to
guide them.

It's true that there is nothing new under the sun. Nor
under the covers. Ovid's *Ars Amatoria* (*The Art of Love*) and *Remedia Amoris* (*Remedies of Love*) prove that our obsession with
love, relationships, and sex is ancient history. *Ars Amatoria*, a
didactic poem in three parts, took courtship and eroticism
as its central themes. In the first part, Ovid tells men how
to land a woman, and in the second, how to retain her. The
third part addresses women directly, explaining how to find
a guy and not lose him. Conscious that all in this world is
transient, Ovid instructed his readers how to end love affairs in *Remedia Amoris*. These books received tremendous
attention in Ovid's lifetime and for many centuries after.
And in these swatches of history, threads connected ancient
Egypt's sebayts, ancient Greek and Roman philosophers,

and modern-day self-help, the target of my disdain. While the themes were consistent, the form shifted over time. As a bookseller, I learn from my customers. As a student of literature, I wasn't sure I could cast aside my biases to learn anything. Then again, my friend Yasmin always says, "Why would life give you a gentle nudge if it can hit you over the head with a sledgehammer instead?"

"Take these. Once you've read them, we'll need to discuss," ordered Nehaya, our multimedia and stationery buyer, and (in typical Diwan fashion) Nihal's younger cousin.

"What the fuck are these? And why are you handling books now?" I asked.

"I'm not. I bought these for you. You're a disaster and you need help," she said, placing two books on my desk and leaving the office. I examined her gifts: *The Rules* and *Why Men Love Bitches*. I skimmed the blurbs on the back, and then the tables of contents. Sure, I was a little out of my element, but to call me a disaster felt unfair. I just needed time. Number One and I had divorced a year ago. Shit! It was three years ago. Still, he was the last man I'd gone out with, and that had happened before I had a cell phone. Since then, I had wholly thrown myself into Diwan's expansion. I worked constantly, my strategy for mending my broken heart and filling the gap left by my marriage—I had really become Mrs. Diwan. I dreamed about the bottom line. I saw red everywhere. In my waking life, I was busy brainstorming our annual marketing plan, overseeing the purchasing and restocking of English titles, and parenting a five- and a seven-year-old. Dating was beyond my bandwidth.

But there was no escape from Nehaya's persistence. She took after Nihal in that way. Her name in Arabic literally

means "the end" or "ending." There was an appropriate finality, an impatience, in her affect. She was aggressive and
unapologetic by nature, and she could outtalk anyone. She
had wiry brown hair, a nose stud, and menacing eyes perfect
for staring down suppliers and colleagues. She was mechanical in her efficiency and resilient in her life.

One evening, a few days later, Nehaya invited me to meet
for an ostensibly spontaneous drink.

"Tell me about your progress." She launched into the
subject without preliminaries, assuming I would understand her inquiry immediately, which, admittedly, I did.

"I've skimmed."

"That's not good enough. You have to really read them.
And you have to obey them. You can't be so skeptical or
halfhearted. You have to play by their rules."

"You, and your cousin, are unbelievable!" Nehaya looked
unfazed. "The last time someone gave me a self-help book,
I divorced him." It's true: I have never sought out self-help
books, but for some reason they keep being thrust upon
me. During the final years of our marriage, Number One
bought me a copy of Richard Carlson's *Don't Sweat the Small
Stuff . . . and It's All Small Stuff*, because he felt that Diwan
was bringing too much stress into our marriage. At first, I
was offended. Then I read it. It worked, and I was furious.
I couldn't pinpoint when I'd become such a control freak. I'd
always been filled with dread about the utter uncertainty of
life. Control was a useful fallacy. It allowed me to maintain
a sense of agency. Carlson argued that controlling people,
like me, become perfectionists due to our fragile egos. We
can't tolerate being wrong, criticized, or weak. We lose our
sense of perspective in the process and everything takes
on equal importance: from laundry to taxes to broken
bones to burst pipes. Any deviation from our plans becomes

catastrophic. The book advocated for simple changes, like doing one thing at a time. It provided mental tools for aggravating situations, like imagining people who annoyed you as babies in diapers. For the duration of time that I was conscious of my own thoughts and actions, the advice of not sweating the small stuff had worked. Then, as with most people and most self-help books, I stopped being mindful and the guidance stopped working. But it does work for long enough to convince us of its success and our potential.

"That's not why you got divorced. And anyway, it's been a few years," said Nehaya unhelpfully.

"Nehaya, I'm a feminist. I can't—"

"Shut up. I don't care. I'm a feminist, too. And guess what? There's not a fucking manifesto that says we can't read books about landing guys."

"I'm not one of these women who can't live without a man."

"I didn't say you were. But the dating scene has changed. Why don't you read about it so you can better control it?" She forged ahead. "These books changed my life. They will interrupt your bad habits and bad behavior."

"You know I'm suspicious of easy wisdom."

"Get over it and help yourself."

"What if this particular self is beyond help?" I semi-joked, getting up to refill our glasses. I couldn't admit what I really feared: that I, and everyone else, was beyond redemption. That the self-help genre was created to assuage, and conceal, the deep-seated alienation of being alive under capitalism, under patriarchy, under all other broken systems. That individual self-improvement is a misguided antidote to our increasing isolation from nature, family, and community. Still, I'm not immune to the pleasure of buying something, even if I know it won't fix my larger problem. My vitamin cabinet is full of supplements promising limber tendons, stronger nails, and improved immunity. I have yet to swallow one of those pills.

Diwan's self-help customers flocked to titles that promised painless healing. I remember one interaction perfectly. "I am so happy that I don't have to bring these books back from America anymore. My husband loves Diwan because he doesn't have to pay excess baggage when we travel," gushed a customer as she glossed over a selection of Chicken Soup for the Soul titles. Ahmed, still one of Diwan's best booksellers, newly promoted to customer-service supervisor, stood two paces to her side, his hands clasped behind his back. I watched her eyes dart from cover to cover along the table. Finally, the veiled woman ventured: "I've read all these. What other titles do you have?"

"Excuse me while I check," said Ahmed apologetically. He took it as a personal slight when a customer left Diwan empty-handed.

"I'll try to make your life easier. I have everything they've published until 2008."

"You're a dedicated reader."

"I am. I've always been a deep person. My husband says I have the best taste in books."

"Your husband is a man of vision. But if you don't mind me saying, I think you should share these books with more people. They're restorative, and when we come upon something that heals, it's our responsibility to spread the word." I listened to Ahmed as he gently persuaded the customer that it was her *civic duty* to share the insights of Chicken Soup with her community. "Instead of going to someone's house with sweets or flowers, you should gift them *good vibes*. They will be in your debt forever." I felt vague awe from my hiding place behind an adjacent shelf. Once he had escorted the merry client to the cashier with her purchases, he returned to the main book area, giving me a mock salute.

As Diwan had grown, I'd been slowly replaced by a whole team of buyers. I wasn't ordering or selling books so much as supervising. Ahmed was their filter and their feeder. He talked to customers in stores, gauged their needs, missing titles, new trends, fading fads, and he communicated his findings to the buyers. He suggested we increase our self-help orders. I snapped back, "Why don't we just throw in the couch and the shrink, and change our license from bookstore to psychiatrist?"

Later, back at my desk, I looked up Chicken Soup for the Soul titles. I realized it was more than a book series. It was an empire. There were 250 titles that had sold more than 110 million combined copies in the U.S. and Canada alone. I learned that it was the most successful trade paperback series of all time. This empire had humble origins. In 1993, its founders, two motivational speakers, had set out to gather and publish tales of everyday people overcoming adversity. This project would mutate and expand over time, encompassing a slew of branded products generating more than two billion dollars in retail sales, including, in 2004, a pet food.

The books themselves seemed harmless enough: preachy and ingratiating, sure, but anodyne. But the exponential growth of branded content disturbed me. It seemed in direct contradiction to the folksy, soothing stories the books sold. Flashback to the franchiser who wouldn't shake my female hand. He'd painted a picture of mini-Diwans, stand-alone cafés, flagships in malls, university stores, and seasonal outlets. We'd rejected him, but maybe we'd fulfilled his vision. Chicken Soup for the Soul seemed to symbolize the perverse, but profitable, end result of such an expansion. Despite targeting myriad audiences—beach lovers, NASCAR watchers, menopausal women, golfers, and followers of primarily Western religions—they have never published a collection for Hindus, Buddhists, or Muslims. I wonder if the veiled customer knew, or cared.

Sometimes, walking through the aisles of Diwan, I would look at all our books through the self-help lens. *Pride and Prejudice* becomes a quirky how-to-land-a-guy manual. The *Iliad* is a mirror-of-princes morality tale. The *Arabian Nights* is a literal survival guide. Context is everything. Take one of Diwan's bestselling titles, a crossover from fiction to self-help: Paulo Coelho's *The Alchemist*. I found the author annoying. His books—à la Chicken Soup—were constantly propagating into branded goods and knickknacks, from calendars to diaries to mini-hardbacks of soulful quotations that besieged every holiday season. Of course Nihal loved him. Of course that made me despise him more. Customers kept buying him, which forced me to increase my order quantities and suggested that maybe I didn't know my customers and my market as well as I thought. In the spirit of learning from others and wanting to know what all the fuss was about, I decided to read him.

As with my previous purchase of *What to Expect When You're Expecting*, I disavowed any link to *The Alchemist*, protesting my personal shopper status to the cashier once more. When I got home that evening, I had dinner with Zein and Layla, reread their favorite installment of Captain Underpants to them, tucked them in amid repeated cries for an encore, and then settled down to my own required reading for the night. I turned the cover and flipped through the first pages, debating whether to skip the preface. I settled on a quick skim, pausing at the words "In the course of this book I pass on everything I have learned." I panicked at what sounded like oversharing. I just wanted to get through the book, to understand what the hype was all about. No one warned me about seismic revelations and soulful excavation.

The Alchemist tells the story of Santiago, an Andalusian shepherd boy who has a recurring dream. A gypsy fortune-teller interprets the dream, telling him that a treasure awaits him at the ancient pyramids of Egypt. The book chronicles his physical and spiritual journey, at the end of which he realizes that his dream, or his Personal Legend, belongs to something far greater: the soul of the universe.

In the spirit of confessions inscribed on the walls of tombs—famously written as negations—I was not displeased by the book. It is instructive and undemanding, simple and repetitive. Coelho's copious use of *maktub*, the belief in fate and determinism, which literally translates to *it is written*, delighted me, as did the endgame: Santiago's treasure would be found at the ancient Egyptian pyramids of Giza. And like the *khamaseen* winds of the Sahara, my customers' pride in all things Egyptian blew over me, sweeping away my skepticism.

I'd arrived at the book with a set of beliefs that I'd begun to develop in childhood. My parents had drilled in me the conviction that the harder I worked, the better I would be, mentally, spiritually, emotionally, physically, and financially. I developed a disdain for things that came easily. For a moment, the book undid this mindset completely, describing "the language of enthusiasm, of things accomplished with love and purpose, and as part of a search for something believed in and desired." I'd never encountered a better explanation for Diwan. The secret to Hind's, Nihal's, and my success was our love and passion, the essential truth of our shared desire to create something sincere that spoke to us. I had hardly even noticed that passion at the time, as I perused shop floors, stacked books, and introduced customers to their new favorite authors. Now, I noticed it because it was no longer there. It was subsumed by the manic urgency to grow, to multiply. Inevitably, the essence had become diluted. But in the midst of this upheaval, I'd begun to realize how creative and gutsy our commitment to spreading culture in its broadest sense had been. We'd tried so many different formats in so many different locations. We didn't give up until we had to.

By the time I finished the book, the spell had faded. I'd read it to better understand Diwan's readers, and the market, but I finished it still feeling alienated from both. Good books, I feel, should inquire, suggest, and probe our fixed notions, without giving us new ones. As a student of literature, I had feasted on Hermann Hesse's *Steppenwolf* and James Joyce's *Ulysses*. Literature of sustenance and nourishment. Self-help was like Pringles. It required no work to enjoy. This made it popular. Another one of our bestsellers, Steven W. Anderson's *Passing Time in the Loo*, a collection of summaries of classics, also let readers cheat, and sacrificed nuance for ease. But in that case, I didn't mind—because it didn't promise spiritual healing or guidance; it didn't conceal its own reason for being. As a bookseller, I had a duty to challenge and broaden readers' horizons. As a business owner, I owed my partners the deepest margins and the highest sales volumes that I could generate. As a passionate reader, I was allowed to inhabit the latitudes of love and hate.

It didn't help that I'd met Paulo Coelho years before. In 2005, he visited Egypt and lectured at Cairo University. Photographs of him seated next to Naguib Mahfouz flooded newspapers. Diwan, as his designated bookseller, shepherded him through every venue, selling hundreds of his books along the way. Finally, near the end of his visit, I was seated next to him at a dinner. I immediately told him how much I'd enjoyed a recent lecture of his at Cairo University. He was completely uninterested, probably so accustomed to cultish reverence that my enthusiasm left no impression. He turned to the lady on his other side, and I left.

The exchange, like most exchanges with people we have only met in our minds, was disappointing. By 2014, his book had been on the *New York Times* bestseller list for more than 315 weeks, had been translated into eighty different languages, and held the Guinness world record for the most translated book by any living author. By 2014, I had been stocking and stacking the shelves of Diwan's ten stores for over a decade. I was getting worn out. I sent a memo to the buying department banning *The Alchemist*, and all other Paulo Coelho titles, from our display tables, unless they were newly released. I was tired of walking into Diwans, only to be greeted by *Veronika* deciding to die, or *Eleven Minutes*, or *The Witch of Portobello*. I worried my buyers were getting lazy. They were supposed to support and uphold Diwan's mission of surprising and delighting our customers with new books. Paulo's books began to symbolize the path of least resistance: they pledged certainty to a world of uncertainty.

"What the hell is he doing over there?"

"Don't raise your voice; we're in a bookstore," Dalia hissed, her hands up in a pacifying gesture. Dalia, Diwan's head buyer, had been mentored and trained by the formidable Nehaya, and it showed.

"I'll calm down if you explain this abomination." I stared her down. We were in the new Maadi store, located on Road 254. We'd opened it in 2013, a few years after closing our original Maadi location, which had failed miserably. During our expansion phase, we'd made big mistakes: we opened shops in locations that weren't ideal, then closed them too early, or kept them open too long. Both outcomes added to the losses on our balance sheet. We wrote them off generously and overrated the benefits of the lessons they taught. As with our successes, Hind, Nihal, and I divided our disasters equally among ourselves. We cared too much about one another's feelings to hurt them. I knew serious businessmen wouldn't have taken the same care. But we weren't serious, and we weren't men.

"Is this about your memo? This is a new title, so it can be displayed on main tables according to your rule."

"Five months old hardly qualifies as 'new' in our industry."

As we kept arguing, I was reminded of just how much control I'd ceded over the years to Dalia and her team of buyers. I'd given up what I loved the most. Dalia had worked at Diwan for a decade, risen through the ranks, and now held one of the most critical jobs in the administration. I knew she was more adept with numbers and spreadsheets than I, but I still insisted on looking over her shoulder at every turn, checking the numbers of her copious reports.

"I think you should showcase more original authors," I urged.

"More than I already do?" Dalia shuffled through yet another report. "Let's see. Hilary Mantel's *Bring Up the Bodies* has only sold ten copies of the fifty I ordered over the last nine months."

"Maybe because you gambled on the hardback. You know this isn't a hardback market," I interjected unhelpfully.

"You can't give us budgets and targets, then keep us from achieving them."

"Put them on the central display table and brief customer-service staff to recommend them." At this point, I was pleading.

"Nehaya taught me that every title pays rent to sit on my shelf. If it doesn't pay, it gets evicted," Dalia retorted, as we were joined by Sayed, her assistant. His gaze shifted between Dalia and me. He clearly had no interest in adjudicating on a disagreement between his boss and her boss. She continued, "Just because it won the Man Booker doesn't mean our readers care."

"Bookselling is like marriage and football. While a fair amount of skill is needed, it's more about fate, and luck, than we'd like to admit." I paused, then offered a bargain. "I'll give you Paulo, if you give me Hilary, right next to him."

"Deal. They get one month, and then they're both off the table." Dalia nodded to Sayed, who noted our concessions to each other in his notebook with the quiet demeanor of a scribe.

Self-help books tend to mirror the ailments of the eras in which they are written. After the 2008 crash and subsequent depression, books of financial guidance proliferated. In the consumerism and abundance that followed, the decluttering guru Marie Kondo flourished. Despite my resentment of the popular self-help genre, I believe books do help us. In the decade before the Egyptian revolution, self-help sales soared. Whether due to correlation or causation, these unprecedented sales felt related to the genre's promise of agency and problem-solving. Egyptians, tired of waiting for the government to help them, looked for arenas where they could help themselves. It was better than doing nothing.

Over Diwan's first decade, customers browsing the Arabic section of our stores bought pragmatic how-to books to better their skills as vibrant members of the labor force. These books upheld the belief that our lives can improve if we work harder. The Arabic translation of Stephen Covey's *The 7 Habits of Highly Successful People* sold remarkably well. I wondered if Diwan's readers shared my ambivalence toward these Western business books, which so clearly targeted an audience that didn't include us.

I'd given up entirely on reading them. Instead, following Nihal's recommendation, I read about positive thinking. I tried to manifest, to visualize, to focus. At the end of every quarter, I willed the next quarter to be better. But it never was, no matter what we did. Our cycles of success, failure, profit, and loss were difficult to break. As we sank further into the red, Hind, Nihal, and I discussed pathways that could take us back into the black. Nihal said we had to close more stores. Hind believed we had to keep on going till we made ends meet. I didn't know what to think. I was tired. My dream was distant and unmanageable. Diwan felt like an albatross hanging around my neck. I worried that Diwan was retaliating against us for wanting too much and taking too much. But we kept each other afloat. Some days, Nihal felt it was hopeless; other days I did. Hind reminded us that all was transient.

Just as we'd expanded, we began to aggressively contract. We closed stores and laid off staff. We paid out penalties and granted early-termination packages. The first store to go was Mohandiseen. I wasn't too attached to it, so it didn't sting, unlike Cairo University. That was the failure that I couldn't call anything else. I still wished I could have re-envisioned the space differently, like making it just a café with some affordable stationery items. My tunnel vision had kept me from seeing what was. Next were the smaller locations, like the kids' Diwan inside the Gezira Sporting Club (encouraged by the growing number of potential bookstores, they had decided to double the rent), then the mall stands. The Cairo Airport Diwan had languished under bureaucracy. Government rules and regulations had kept us from doing our jobs. We were allowed to deliver our merchandise to their warehouses, but we were not permitted to restock in the store. Instead, we had to trust duty-free staff who did nothing without constant harassment and cajoling.

Finally, we made a plan: we would simplify our existing stores. We couldn't rebuild our vision for every neighborhood or every new customer base. We had to make a formula and trust it. But if one thing disrupts a tidy business plan, it's massive political tumult. Like a car crash, it happened both instantly and in slow motion. On January 25, 2011, Egyptians filled public squares. Their frustration at every unfulfilled promise made over the previous five decades was palpable. During the early days, before we could call it a revolution, there was a series of escalating protests that police responded to with rubber bullets and tear gas. I called my mother.

"Mum, it's not safe for you to stay alone. Move in with us, at least until we see how this will turn out."

"My darling, you remind me of your father. Always worrying. I'm relieved he is no longer with us. He'd be having a fit with all this uncertainty, and I'd have to listen to him rant."

"Mum, you shouldn't be alone."

"I'm not alone, and neither is Egypt. *Masr Mahrousa*. Egypt is blessed. It always has been, and it always will be. Everything is as it should be. It will all work out in the end."

"Mum, look out of your fucking window. Do you not see the tear gas?"

"Your problem is that you rely too much on what you see."

Revolutions are cataclysmic. Emotions run high. Discontent and hope flourish side by side. Ancient fault lines break open. Nothing is tidy. Nothing is clear. As an Egyptian observing the events of 2011, I felt tentatively optimistic. As a business owner, I dreaded the cost of anarchy. Unless you are a volatility index in the stock market, instability doesn't make you money. And the months of instability that followed were emotionally and financially destructive. Marches and protests erupted in every city. We tried to keep staff morale and physical stores intact. For our remaining seven stores and 108 staff members, the protests, curfews, and blocked roads added to the uncertainty. Every day, we lost revenue. Stores couldn't open. People were buying food, not books. Aware of our social responsibilities, and regardless of cash flow and battered balance sheets, we continued to pay full salaries while many other businesses deferred or withheld payment.

Like an agnostic praying to God in times of need, I

found myself wishing that there were a self-help book to guide me through what I was feeling. Under Mubarak's reign, Egypt had been riddled with injustice. But we were accustomed to that injustice. Now, we feared the unknown. As unrest continued, protests became *millioniyat*, million-man marches. Tahrir Square was the focal point. I knew the area well. I'd walked through it daily as a university student. I'd rescued *The Naked Chef* from the nearby Mogamma'.

So many others were spending their days and nights in the square. Forming a utopian microcosm. Helping others. Dreaming of a different country. I'd dreamed of a different country in the 1990s, protesting against female genital mutilation. This time, I didn't protest. I didn't go to Tahrir Square because none of the factions seemed to represent my hopes for Egypt. I wasn't sure what anyone stood for.

And I had a business to run. Even though we weren't making profits, we were still a third place. Our shop floors became confessionals. People gathered, spoke, and compared experiences. Diwan was a place to escape from, or return to, the political moment. I asked myself difficult questions. What was Diwan's role in all of this? How would we adapt to survive? There was one question I couldn't even ask myself: Would Diwan survive at all?

After eighteen days and nights of protests, President Hosni Mubarak stepped down, bringing his thirty-year reign to an end. There was euphoria at the bright future that lay ahead. By 2012, following a year of transitional governments, political naïveté (we should have read *The Prince* more closely), and chaos, we found ourselves between a rock and a hard place. We were finally back at the ballot boxes, forced to

choose between two familiar candidates: a Muslim Brotherhood candidate and an ex-army general. Like the spinning
earth, we were back where we started.

On June 30, 2012, almost a year and a half after the first
protests, Mohamed Morsi, the Muslim Brotherhood candidate, was sworn in as Egypt's first democratically elected
president. Morsi would be a president to some Egyptians,
but not all. Not me. My staff and I were divided. They sympathized with the Brotherhood for practical if not religious
reasons. Most had grown up in areas where Brotherhood
community organizations offered education and medical
services that far surpassed the meager government offerings. I resented past governments for having delivered their
people to Islamists by failing to meet their most basic needs.

In another context, I would have sucked it up and endured.
One or two terms and he's gone. Unfortunately, that's not
how Egypt's rulers operate. They abdicate only under pressure from the hand of God or the boot of man. I dreaded
decades of Islamic rule for Egypt. I knew I couldn't change
the inevitable. Once again, I could control only myself. I
planned my exodus. When, a year later, Morsi and his ca-
bal were ousted by popular revolt and army boots, my plans
had already begun. I heard the banter in our office corridors, Muslim staff "joking" with their Coptic colleagues
that they hoped they would be spared the *jizya*, a tax historically paid by non-Muslims to their Muslim rulers. I wasn't
laughing. I had to choose between Diwan's future and my
children's, and I chose the latter. Diwan had already claimed
the last fifteen years.

Our customers were reading more than ever. While sales
of my English books fell—buying them seemed almost
unpatriotic—Hind's Arabic sales mushroomed. The early

revolution years produced infinite material for sarcasm, sat-
ire, and absurdism, all of which flourished in the newfound
disorder and freedom from censorship. Talk shows rode the
wave. Everyone had an opinion and insisted on voicing it.
So everyone talked and nobody listened. As quickly as the
tornado of overexpression swept through Egypt, it consumed itself, spinning out into nothing.

Around 2014, buying patterns shifted as collective fa-
tigue set in, eventually giving way to disillusionment. There
was a notably increased demand for spiritual titles. I felt
the pain of our disappointment. Books, especially books
about transcendence, were antidotes to burnout. We'd been
watching the news too much in the fevered years following
the revolution. There was a sense of impending failure. The
Arab Spring had unspooled into the endless winter of our
discontent. Suddenly, everyone seemed to be buying the
2008 translation of Rhonda Byrne's *The Secret*, a book about
manifesting one's desires through the power of thought.
After my tryst with Paulo, and at Nihal's behest, I picked
it up, read the first few pages, and instinctively understood
what it promised. The Bible made a similar vow, in the Gos-
pel of Luke, "for everyone who asks receives; he who seeks
finds; and to him who knocks the door will be opened."
The Alchemist and *The Secret* spoke to a quintessentially human habit: dreaming. We wanted to make our dreams real.
But what happens after that? When your dream comes true,
outgrowing what you've imagined, what then? There's the
problem of classification. A dream cannot materialize, or it
no longer is itself. Maybe the entelechy of dreams could be
called loss.

We wanted to remake ourselves. We wanted to remodel
our country. We wanted to know one another. We kept the
faith, despite the odds. We refused to be bitter. Reading

itself is an expression of faith, if not the ultimate act of self-help.

"I have a present for you," I said to Nihal, as I placed a copy of Paul Arden's *It's Not How Good You Are, It's How Good You Want to Be* between her hands.

"I thought you hated self-help books." Nihal's eyes sparkled with surprise.

"I wouldn't go so far as hate. Besides, it's not a self-help book. It's from Art and Design. It's by an advertising guru . . . charlatans who know they are charlatans. My kind of people." I knew Nihal would need convincing. I took back the book and began flipping through its pages, reading aloud. "'Your vision of where or who you want to be is the greatest asset you have.' Fucking brilliant. 'Without having a goal it is difficult to score.' Fucking genius. 'The perosn'—intentionally misspelled—'who doesn't make mistakes is unlikely to make anything.' Fucking true. We are living proof. And my fucking favorite: 'Fail. Fail again. Fail better.'" I could tell she was sold. I handed the book back.

That last line was excerpted from my favorite pessimist, Samuel Beckett. I lived by his words. "Ever tried. Ever failed. No matter. Try again. Fail again. Fail better." The line has a strange life of its own, appearing tattooed on the arm of a famous tennis player and in the online bios of multiple Silicon Valley techies. In case you're wondering, it applies to everything, the best and the worst in this life: love, marriage, business, friendship, revolutions, and even hope.

EPILOGUE

When I left Cairo, feeling broken and beaten, I kept returning to the days when Diwan was simpler. When Hind, Nihal, and I were all positive forces in each other's lives. When I wasn't crippled by guilt for abandoning everyone and everything I held dear. I felt like a fraud whenever anyone congratulated me on what we'd built. Money may not be the most important measure of success, but in business it is. The truth is that Diwan isn't a business. She's a person, and this is her story.

If I had the chance to do it all again, I would never prioritize income over impact. I would choose a bookstore that made a mark over a bookstore that made a profit. We had to make mistakes in order to learn from them. We had to pay a steep price for doing what hadn't been done before. Maybe we should've been satisfied with just one shop. But Zamalek was always too small for all of us.

The first five years were chaos. Somehow, things went according to the plan we hadn't even made. The next five years deviated wildly from the plans we did make. And the five years after that were just painful. Nihal, depleted, went on leave from Diwan. Hind and I followed. But we couldn't leave Diwan with no one. We tried to appease her. We created a five-person management team from the different divisions. It didn't go well. We hired a CEO. It went less well.

Finally, the world aligned in a way that agreed with Diwan. Nihal had maintained a close friendship with two ex-Diwaners. One, Amal, had taken over from Shahira as Zamalek's manager for a few years, and the other, Layal, had been the assistant manager of Heliopolis. Even after both left Diwan, they continued to meet up with Nihal in Diwan's cafés throughout the city. They reminisced about old times. They wondered, "What if?" And slowly, a new trinity formed. Nihal, the eternal believer in partnerships, was energized by their shared vision, oriented toward the future rather than the past. It was a happy coincidence of friendship and passion. In 2017, Nihal, Amal, and Layal joined Diwan's board. The following year, to make space for this new vision, Hind and I offered our resignations. For the first time since we founded Diwan in 2001, we weren't board members.

Where is everyone now? We lost some of them. During our early years, we coddled our staff and their brittle egos. As time passed, we became less tolerant. If any staff member threatened to resign, we would enact their threat then and there. We insisted that we were all part of the Diwan family, but we reminded staff that no one was indispensable. Samir, after ten years as my driver, threatened to leave. I don't remember exactly what pushed him over the edge. His thick skin generally insulated him from anything I could've said or done. Nonetheless, he made the threat. I cut the cord. It was definitely long overdue. He calls every Christmas to ask about Zein and Layla. He advises me to strike a balance with my daughters between affection and discipline, as he knows that I can be a little rough-mannered. He tells me that his years building Diwan were among the most rewarding of his life.

Then there was Amir, book procurer extraordinaire. He was Diwan's first employee. He had worked his way to head of Arabic-book buying, developing his own team of assistant buyers and data analysts. After fifteen years, he left to start his own publishing house. He broke the news to Hind, Nihal, and me with typical flattery: "This is your victory. You taught me everything I know. I'm continuing your work." We wished him luck. In a gesture that defied social, gender, and class conventions, he kissed each of our foreheads. I cried. Hind read the gesture as the promise of a son not to let his mother down. When we told our mother about it later, she saw Judas and Jesus. I'd attended his first marriage and his second marriage, and paid my respects when his father died. Still, we never quite transcended our boss/employee dynamic. I knew him very well, and I didn't know him at all.

Readers left remnants of themselves on our shelves. They took remnants away, too, in books and bags. While the bitter end of the Diwan bag changed Minou's and my relationship forever, we remain friends. She continued to pursue her passion for photography and mixed media. She had several international exhibitions, and her work was ac- quired by London's Victoria and Albert Museum and Am- sterdam's Tropenmuseum. She lived between London and Cairo for several years before deciding to return to Cairo. She found that she couldn't create work outside Egypt. The country was her muse.

Loss is a natural process, and sometimes even a joyous one. During Nehaya's stint as multimedia and stationery buyer, she met a man named Dany, the general manager of a distribution company. He had an inextinguishable joie de vivre and could miraculously outtalk the gregarious Nehaya. I witnessed their first meeting, where he was trying to sell her stock and she was demanding a better discount. They realized they couldn't intimidate each other. I left the room. I sent Nehaya's then assistant, Dalia, to get Nehaya and bring her to me, under the guise of a "pricing emergency."

"He's flirting with you," I said.

"What?"

"Flirt back. He's nice. He's funny. He's not scared of you."

"I don't have time for this shit." Nehaya rolled her eyes at me.

"Neither do I, but it doesn't stop you making me read books about dating. Practice what you fucking preach." I pointed her in the direction of the door with a warning, "Remember, I'll be watching." They married a year later. Dany got a job in Saudi Arabia. Nehaya left Diwan to join him. I hosted a dinner to celebrate their wedding.

"God help the poor bastard," said Hind, watching Nehaya and Dany from across the room.

"For moving or marrying?" I asked.

"Marrying Nehaya. He's going to need God and his fucking army," chimed in Nihal, as we clinked glasses in agreement. Finally, I had persuaded Nihal of something: a well-placed swear word.

When I left Egypt, Egypt also left me. In London, I tried to find a job in bookselling, only to discover that a Cairo bookseller was an exotic proposition as long as she stayed in Cairo and ordered English books for the natives to read. Her experience didn't translate. The English market was apparently much more sophisticated. I thought readers were readers everywhere. I was gutted, and I was furious.

"Darling, what I am about to say will ease your discomfort and set you free," my mother said with somber gravitas. "You are nothing. Accept it. Embrace it."

"Mum, you do know that I already feel like shit?"

"Be grateful that doors are closing. Others will open. Be humble. Accept being knocked down. Detach. You are nothing, and from nothing comes everything."

"I don't know what kind of shit you've been reading, but please stop."

"It's a fabulous book that Nihal gave me."

Speaking of closed doors: Number Two and I had met in 2009. I was sure that this time I had gotten it right. We married in 2010. Five years on, with my recent move to London, and his work in Dubai, we found ourselves in a commuter marriage. It survived for another year. Then, in the summer of 2016, on our way out of a Bruce Springsteen concert, he suggested we divorce. (Once a die-hard fan, I can now listen to only two Springsteen songs.) He returned to Dubai. Zein and Layla were flying back from their summer vacation with Number One in the United States. I checked the time, waited to ensure that they were safely on the plane, then called him, planning to discuss how best to tell them.

"I'm glad you called. There's something I need to talk to you about," Number One gushed.

"Me, too. What's up?"

"I'm getting divorced. I need to tell the girls."

"Again? Are you fucking serious? So am I. Fuck. Fuck. Fuck!"

"There are worse things than divorce."

"Do you realize that between us we will now have six divorces? You four. Me two. What kind of example are we setting?"

"Resilience. Endurance. It doesn't matter. What matters to Zein and Layla is that we're okay. So, put on some makeup, maybe some heels, go and pick them up from the airport, and look happy. Be happy. Trust me. I know what I'm talking about." Number One was right.

A week later, I flew to Dubai, met Number Two at the Egyptian consulate, and signed the divorce papers. I took the next flight back to London, in time to take Zein and Layla to the West End theater production of *Aladdin*. I wished I could have put the genie back in the lamp. I didn't want a second divorce. My problem was with the number, not the action. I could justify the first divorce: I hadn't known any better. But the second? Either there was something wrong with me, or I just really sucked at matrimony. After two pregnancies, I got my tubes tied. After two divorces, I made the vow: never again. Number One made the same vow. A few years after the revolution, he moved back to America; became a serial monogamist; continued to teach history, play in a rock band, and obsess over his daughters' academic and social lives; and has now started writing his first novel. After reading this memoir, he told me that I'd written my very own self-help book.

When I started writing, I didn't want to write the story of Diwan. Hind agreed that it was a terrible idea. She suggested I do it anyway. The writing of this book has been an exorcism of sorts. After twenty years as Mrs. Diwan, I hope I've managed to get divorced, which, as I learned, is not the same thing as failing.

———

If Zamalek is on an island in the middle of a river surrounded by a desert, England is also on an island, one with shit weather. On this island, I feel like neither an immigrant nor part of a diaspora. When I was sixteen, I read Camus's *The Outsider*. I saw myself in the title. Today, the knowledge that I don't belong anywhere liberates me. The books on Diwan's shelves stayed in place and moved, were bought and left behind. I see myself in them.

London became my home primarily because Hind had moved here. After fifteen years in Diwan's kitchen, with too many cooks and three head chefs, she came here to go to culinary school. When she graduated from Leiths School of Food and Wine, then Le Cordon Bleu, friends asked her if she wanted to be a chef. She'd demurely reply that she was a *cook*. I thought of Fatma and Abla Nazeera, and I chided her for making herself smaller than she is.

Hind has moved on from Diwan. When she visits Cairo, she spends a lot of time in her garden. In an unconscious nod to Voltaire, and under the experienced eye of Abbas, her driver of the last twenty years, Hind started planting herbs, then vegetables. Last Christmas in Cairo, she presented me with one fruit of her labors: a watermelon the size of an orange. I suggested she fail better. She has. "We must go and work in the garden," *Candide* reminds us. The value of hard work instilled in us by our father makes this life, with its disappointments, bearable.

My relationship with Diwan is more fluid than Hind's. I cherish Diwan without attachment, as I do Number One. Like motherhood, Diwan made me and then broke me. More important, Hind, Nihal, and I have maintained a relationship that exists outside of Diwan, regardless of Diwan. Nihal has read drafts of this book. For once, she had something in common with Minou. I sought their blessing. Nihal was Nihal: "I trust you. If that is how you saw it and felt it, then that is how you must write it." And Minou was Minou: "Just because you are some fucking fascist bitch doesn't mean I am. In life, people tell you what you can and can't say. I stick to art." I don't own this story. I only own my point of view.

Whenever I return to Cairo, I shop at Diwan. When Ahmed finds me on any of the shop floors, he feels compelled to try out his upselling techniques. I curb my instinct to adjust displays or rearrange books in alphabetical order; I do not wish to trespass. I don't shop for books at my old haunts. Hag Mustafa and Hag Madbouli both passed away. Their sons have continued in their footsteps, taking over the family businesses. Even the Mogamma', Cairo's memory palace, closed down, its many departments redistributed to different administrations throughout the city and to a new capital being built on the outskirts of Cairo. Rumor has it that it will be repurposed into a luxury hotel. Bookstores opened and closed. Chains were built and dismantled. Diwan still stands. On March 8, 2022, the Zamalek store turns twenty.

Sometimes I wonder if loss is contagious. After my father's death, I talked to him. Twenty years on, I still talk to him. The world he tried to prepare us for delivered the ugliness he had anticipated, as well as the beauty he had forgotten. Immediately after his death, we felt a hollowness in our lives. We looked for ways to fill it. Diwan filled it. Diwan's shelves continued to supply his lessons, and other lessons in love, life, and dreams.

Every year, my mother, Hind, and I visit his grave at the foot of the Mokattam hills, and we scatter tuberose and red roses on the ground above where we had laid him to rest. Going, I collected the stories I wanted to share: I have four bookstores, I have seven bookstores, they're now ten, back to seven. You have two granddaughters, I think I failed at marriage, but I succeeded at divorce. Twice. My mother takes out her rosary and prays for his soul. Hind explains to Ramzi and Murad where we are and what it symbolizes. I tell Zein and Layla to share their funny stories; their grandfather loved hearing tales of outspoken girls giving to this world as good as they got.

Diwan was nine years old in 2011, when Cairo erupted. She was eleven in 2013, when Mohamed Morsi, Egypt's first democratically elected president, was removed from power. She was fifteen years old when Nihal returned and revitalized her, with the help of two new business partners. My mother was right. *Egypt is blessed.*

ACKNOWLEDGMENTS

There is so much to be grateful for; and so many to be grateful to . . .

Caroline Dawnay, super-agent, at United Agents for her appetite for risk and her resilience.

Kat Aitken at United Agents for being this book's most vocal advocate.

Georgina Le Grice, Lucy Joyce, Alex Stephens, and the fantastic team of foreign-rights agents who made so many translations of *Shelf Life* possible.

Mitzi Angel at Farrar, Straus and Giroux for seeing a narrative in the midst of anecdotes and recollections, and for believing in this book and its storyteller.

Molly Walls for editing the fuck out of *Shelf Life* and for teaching me how to write, and more important how to cut. I will miss our exchanges in the margins of so many drafts. FM/AM.

To everyone else at FSG, especially Hannah Goodwin, Na Kim, Lauren Roberts, Songhee Kim, and Peter Richardson.

To all the women who were impossible and yet made so much possible: the mentors, the difficult women I fought with, and the friends. You know who you are.

Samer El-Karanshawy and Ragia Omran for answering

endless questions about language, laws, political movements, and history.

Amir al-Nagui, Shahira Fathy, Minou Hammam, Nehaya Nashed, and Nihal Schawky for remembering so much of what I had forgotten.

Shahira Diab and Samir Tawfik for their continuous encouragement and for listening to my many rants.

My mother, Faiza, for her quiet wisdom and for always suggesting I soldier on.

My sister, Hind, for being my harshest critic and my savior.

My nephews: Ramzi, for being the grammar police of our family, and Murad, for never giving me the chance to take myself seriously.

My daughters, Zein and Layla, for graciously accepting that my work took time away from them.

Egypt, my first love; and Diwan, my last love. Thank you for breaking me and remaking me.

To all those who made Diwan—her customers and her staff—thank you for everything.